MARK TWAIN AND ME

A Little Girl's Friendship with Mark Twain

Just after our friendship began,
Mark Twain and I posed
for photographers on board
the "S.S. Minnetonka."

MARK TWAIN AND ME

A LITTLE GIRL'S FRIENDSHIP
WITH MARK TWAIN

by Dorothy Quick

University of Oklahoma Press : Norman

by Dorothy Quick

Bold Heart and Other Poems (Washington, D. C., 1960)
Changing Winds (New York, London, 1935)
Cry in the Night (New York, 1959)
Doctor Looks at Murder, The (New York, 1959)
Enchantment: A Little Girl's Friendship
  with Mark Twain (Norman, 1961)
Fifth Dagger, The (New York, 1947)
Interludes (New York, 1953)
Laugh while You Can (New York, 1940)
One Night in Holyrood (Portland, Me., 1949)
Something Evil (New York, 1959)
Spears into Life (New York, London, 1938)
Strange Awakening (New York, 1938)
Threads (New York, 1927)
Too Strange a Hand (New York, 1959)
To What Strange Altar (New York, 1940)
Variations on a Theme (New York, 1947)

Previously published under the title
Enchantment: A Little Girl's Friendship
with Mark Twain.

ISBN:0-8061-1122-4

Library of Congress Catalog Card Number: 61–15143

Copyright 1961 by the University of Oklahoma Press,
Publishing Division of the University.
Composed and printed at Norman, Oklahoma, U.S.A.,
by the University of Oklahoma Press.

3   4   5   6   7   8   9   10   11   12

to Mother

If I could take the roses of a June
Distil their fragrance into magic words
Containing the bright glory of high noon
And sweetest notes of all the singing birds
Then capture gleaming star-dust from the skies
To weave in sentences pristinely new—
With words like these and God to make me wise
I could write verses worthier of you.

Acknowledgments

THE MARK TWAIN LETTERS are published with the permission of the Mark Twain Company, the Estate of Samuel L. Clemens, and Harper and Brothers with full copyright reservations.

I am indebted to Clara Clemens Samossoud and the late Albert Bigelow Paine for their kindness and interest, which made this book possible. Thanks are also due the editors of the *North American Review* for permission to re-publish certain parts of an article they published under the title "A Little Girl's Mark Twain."

DOROTHY QUICK

New York City
July 13, 1961

Contents

Illustrations

MARK TWAIN AND ME

A Little Girl's Friendship with Mark Twain

I

I Meet Mark Twain

A LITTLE GIRL walked round and round the deck of an ocean liner. On the starboard side she fairly flew along, but when she turned the corner and came to the port side of the vessel, she walked slowly and her feet dragged while her eyes were fixed in admiration on a man standing beside the rail talking to another man.

Both men were staring out toward the far horizon. They didn't see the little girl whose gaze was riveted on the older of the two, the man who had a great mass of snow-white hair and a keen, kindly, observant face—Mark Twain!

Only a little while ago he had come on deck, made one or two turns and then paused beside the rail to have the talk with his friend that was now engrossing him.

It was a heaven-sent opportunity for me. I could observe without being observed; and so I commenced my circling of the deck, and as I did so, took in every detail of the figure at the rail until there was no line of the famous face that I did not know.

Mark Twain was not tall. As a matter of fact, I, who was big for my age, came nearly up to his shoulder. But although he wasn't high in the matter of inches, he gave the effect of being tall by his magnificent carriage and the commanding way in which he held his head. He was very straight and his slender shoulders were always well back while his head was invariably held high, so that he seemed much taller than he actually was.

As the weather was cool that first day at sea, he was dressed in gray tweeds with a matching overcoat, and he held in his hands a gray cap. His head was left free to the breeze which whipped his soft white hair about his face until it seemed like an intensified halo.

I was fascinated by that crop of snowy hair. It was soft as the down of a thistle and whiter than the gleaming feathers of a swan. Beneath it was a broad, low forehead from which thick, bushy eyebrows stuck out in a quizzical manner as they over-shadowed piercing blue eyes. Mark Twain's eyes had the clear gaze possessed by men who have followed the sea. They were particularly blue and brilliant—eyes ever alert, that had friendly little laugh wrinkles around their corners.

His skin was as smooth and fresh as a child's, except for two deep furrowed lines on either side of his face which, when he was serious or in repose, gave him rather a stern look that vanished entirely when he talked or smiled. He had a drooping moustache, slightly yellowed at the ends, which almost hid his mouth, and a small chin which did not lack firmness. He wore a low, turned-down collar, and in his hand was a long black cigar which every now and then he would place between his lips and draw upon luxuriously.

I watched every movement that he made, every change of expression on his mobile face as long as I was within radius,

4

and then spent the rest of my walk around the deck impressing all on my memory.

I walked past him five times. On my sixth trip I saw that his companion was gone.

Just as I came abreast of him, he turned suddenly and to my utter amazement held out his hand and said in a slow, drawly voice, "Aren't you going to speak to me, little girl?"

If the boat had suddenly developed wings and flown to the moon, I couldn't have been more astonished!

I put my hand in his and managed to say, "I'd love to," quite articulately through the lump of excitement in my throat.

"Do you know who I am?" There was a twinkle in his blue eyes as he asked the question.

"Of course. You're Mark Twain." I said it as though he were Santa Claus, Solomon, Napoleon, and the Archangel Gabriel welled into one composite figure. For me, he stood for even more than these impressive names.

"Well, as long as you know my name, suppose you tell me yours," he suggested, pulling at his moustache as he spoke.

"Dorothy Quick," I answered—still too excited to be able to do more than reply to his question.

"That's a nice name. Names are very important things, just like words," he said and then swung around until he faced the sea. Because my hand was still in his, I automatically followed his lead.

We both leaned on the rail, and, having discovered I had no thought of running away, he released my hand and began rambling on about the importance of words. He was trying to put me at my ease and dissipate the shyness that still engulfed me.

It didn't seem possible to me that I was actually standing

5

beside the Mark Twain of whom I had heard, read, and dreamed!

Only yesterday I had seen Mark Twain for the first time in a London railroad station. I had been leaning out of the compartment window watching the bustling activity that always attends a boat train when I had caught sight of a crowd of people centered around a man with a great shock of white hair.

"Oh!" I had exclaimed and leaned still farther out of the window. "There's Mark Twain!"

I knew him instantly. There was no mistaking the foremost representative of American literature. The English papers had been full of pictures of him during the entire time I had been in England. Mark Twain had come over to receive a degree from Oxford University, and what he had done and what he had said had been the topic of the day. But I had never thought to actually see him in the flesh, and so I craned my neck in an endeavor to get a better look as he went by.

He was so surrounded by friends, admirers, and reporters that I had only a fleeting glimpse of him as he passed, and then a very good view of his black derby as it vanished up the platform.

"He must be sailing on our boat," my Mother said.

I wanted to get out of the compartment and follow the crowd up the platform, but this idea was promptly discouraged by my family. In order to distract my mind from the exploring possibilities, my grandfather began to tell me how much he admired Mark Twain.

"You know Mark Twain, whose real name is Samuel Langhorne Clemens, is a very remarkable man. I admire him more than any figure of the present age," he said, "not only because he is a great writer, but because of his integrity. When a publishing house, Webster and Company, with which he was associated, failed, Mark Twain insisted that every creditor be paid in full. Legally it wouldn't have been necessary but because he was the soul of honor he accepted the moral responsibility, and literally talked himself out of debt and into fortune again by going on a lecture tour around the world."

The train had started, and I had settled down into my seat eager to hear more. My grandfather continued:

"He was born in Missouri and his parents were of fine stock but poor and simple folk. Samuel Clemens worked from the time he was twelve years old. He set type on a paper his brother owned. He wrote short sketches. Eventually he left Hannibal and tried his hand at many things. He traveled about and finally decided to become a pilot on the Mississippi River. You know all about that, Dorothy, because I've read you the *Life On The Mississippi* which is the record of that phase of his existence."

Indeed I did remember. "What did he do then?" I asked.

"When he left the River, he became a miner. You know about that too, from *Roughing It,* for whatever Samuel Clemens did, he put it into a book later on.

"When he was a miner he amused himself by writing sketches, and he sent them to a paper which published them. The publisher was a far-seeing man and recognized genius, so he offered Sam Clemens a job as editor, where Clemens was an immediate success.

"Then there were a number of years that he combined editorial work and also tried his hand at mining again. During one of these mining excursions he heard the story of the "Jumping Frog" and wrote it. That story literally catapulted him into fame; and after that he did a series of letters that added to his renown.

7

"He took trips to continue the letters for newspapers and that's how *Innocents Abroad* was first published. On the return from the trip, he got the letters together in a book and after that he was firmly established as an author.

"He was also in great demand as a lecturer. It seemed he had achieved every possible success. He associated himself with the publishing house then, and though for a while it was a very successful venture, in the end it crashed and he went on the lecture tour to pay his debts and re-establish himself financially, as I've just told you."

"I'm glad he isn't poor," I said.

My grandfather smiled. "Mark Twain has made and lost several fortunes, but he's got plenty of money now—and not only money, but the love and respect of everyone, and that's more important to have."

"Has he got any little girls?" I asked next.

"His little girls are grown up. He married just after he had established himself as a literary man and had three children, all girls. One of them died and her death was a great blow to him. Later he lost his wife. His other two daughters are still with him. Clara Clemens is a singer and making good on her own account. The other daughter I don't know very much about."

I had admired Mark Twain during the whole of my short life. I had been more or less brought up on his books, for my grandfather, who was a literary person, had told me Mark Twain stories long before I was old enough to have them read to me. To look at him, as a cat might look at a king, or a visitor to an art gallery might regard a rare and precious painting, was the height of my ambition. Just to be on the same boat with him for over a week, to be able to see him every day, to regard him closely, seemed to my young imagination almost too wonderful to be true. And now that I was talking to him, I felt as though I was in the midst of some lovely dream from which I might awaken at any time. It was a thrilling moment.

If I could have looked ahead as I stood beside him at the ship's rail, and seen the letter that Mark Twain would send to Mother after I had made my first visit to him at Tuxedo Park, I wouldn't have believed it possible—not even if some kind genie had appeared with a magic crystal to give me a vision of what was to come. Yet that letter was there, in the future, waiting to be addressed to:

Mrs. Quick,
Plainfield, New Jersey
Courtesy of Dorothy—

> TUXEDO PARK
> NEW YORK
> AUGUST 5/07

Certificate of character from last place.
To all to whom these presents may come, Greetings:
This is to certify that I have been in the service of the enclosed
DOROTHY QUICK
for five days and have found her sober, honest, willing, and unlazy. I desire to further testify that she is always good and sweet and thoughtful of others and winning. Also that she is gentle and considerate of her slaves and never puts a burden upon them that they are not glad to bear. I wish to recommend her in the strongest terms to any worthy free person who is tired of his freedom and desires to exchange it for something better.

(Signed) S. L. CLEMENS

No—if anyone had told me that twenty days later Mark Twain would write that letter I would not have believed it.

9

Nor could the present have held anything more had I known, for just then I felt as though I had reached the height of my dreams.

Mark Twain was talking to me!

After a little while, I lost my awe of him and found my voice, and volunteered the information that I had read all of his books. His bushy eyebrows went up.

"All?" he exclaimed. "That's a pretty big order."

"Oh, yes," I confirmed the sweeping statement which, like the false report of Mr. Clemens' death, was "greatly exaggerated."[1]

Mark Twain, however, was still a trifle incredulous and asked what might be considered a leading question.

"Which did you like best?"

"Tom Sawyer. It's so . . . so . . . ." I groped around for the right word to express what I meant and finally found it. "It's so human!"

I think he was still trying to probe the truth of my claim. I replied promptly.

"The part where Tom gets all his friends to do his work for him. I just loved the way he got that fence white-washed."

Mark Twain threw back his head and laughed heartily. "You know, I always thought that was right smart. Even the day I did it. And I've forgotten how many years ago that was."

"Were you Tom?" I asked wonderingly.

"All the bright things Tom did I took from my own youth; the other things I just made up. Of course, I was never bad."

I didn't know him well enough then to understand that the twinkle in his eyes meant that he was having fun. In truth,

[1] Once, upon hearing of a newspaper's erroneous report of his demise, Mark Twain answered, "You may say that the report of my death has been greatly exaggerated."

10

as he later told me, Tom Sawyer was more or less the story of his younger days, when Tom was both good and bad.

Now my tongue was loosened, and once started it wagged on and on as I described the parts I liked best in *Huckleberry Finn, Connecticut Yankee in King Arthur's Court,* and *Innocents Abroad.*

Finally Mark Twain "allowed" I knew more about his books than he did himself.

The time slipped by unnoticed. Mark Twain got me started telling about myself and we soon made the mutual discovery that we both suffered from bronchitis, which proved a great bond of sympathy.

We talked on and on until the bugle blew announcing luncheon. Then I came down from the high places and remembered that I had a family and that Mother was probably wondering where I was.

"Oh," I cried guiltily, "I must find Mother—she'll be worried about me!"

"That's all right, Dorothy. We'll go find her together and I'll tell her she needn't ever be worried about you when you're with me. She might as well know it now, for we're going to be together a lot, you and I." He said this just as though he were announcing something quite ordinary, instead of opening up an enchanted vista of anticipation.

Hand in hand we walked along the decks of the *S. S. Minnetonka* until we came to the sun deck where my Mother and grandparents had ensconced themselves in a sunshiny corner.

I began to explain my long absence, but Mark Twain said, "I believe you'd better do a little introducing instead." So the explanations were dropped.

Anyway, they weren't necessary. Mother *had* been worried and gone on a searching tour for me. When she had seen whom

I was with, she had returned to her steamer chair to wait for me.

As soon as the introductions had been satisfactorily accomplished, with a great deal of stammering on my part, Mark Twain asked if he could sit with us on deck, and there was a great deal of hustling and bustling among the deck stewards as they set up a steamer chair for him alongside mine.

It was only when we were seated side by side that I actually realized that Mark Twain and I were friends.

2

Shipwreck and Shuffleboard
on the S. S. Minnetonka

I DO NOT THINK THERE was a happier child on land or sea than I was that night as Mother tucked me in my berth.

Just as Mother was about to turn out the light, there was a knock on the door. Before Mother could go across the cabin, the soft drawl I had already grown to know came through.

"Can I come in?"

It was Mark Twain.

I sat up in the narrow berth and called out "Oh, yes, *do* come in," just as Mother swung the door open.

Mark Twain, resplendently clad in a white flannel evening suit, stepped into the cabin.

His face fell as he saw me. "You've gone to bed! My plan's gone too! Someone who knew my fondness for white clothes told me you had on a white sailor suit at dinner, so I came right down to see you in it and show you my suit and how well we go together in our whites!"

"Oh, dear," I said mournfully. "I had my dinner early and

now it's my bedtime so I can't get dressed again! But I can wear my white dress tomorrow." I felt considerably cheered by the prospect. I hated to disappoint my new friend on the first day of our acquaintance.

Mark Twain smiled one of his rare smiles. "That's a promise. Don't you forget! I'll be waiting for you on deck in the morning. Now I guess I can take a hint as well as anyone. It's a certain young lady's bedtime so I am going to say goodnight."

"I didn't mean . . . ." I was distressed, for I hadn't meant for him to go when I said it was my bedtime. In fact, it was an hour I would gladly postpone indefinitely, even if there hadn't been company.

Mark Twain took my hand in his. "I know, dear, but it's good to obey all the rules when you're young so you'll have strength to break them when you are old. Good-night, and don't forget the white suit in the morning. I'll wear mine too!"

A hasty handshake all around and Mark Twain was gone.

In the morning I appeared in my white sailor suit, and it did match Mark Twain's very well. He said he thought it would be a good idea if I wore white the rest of the voyage, "because we're going to be together a lot, Dorothy, and we might as well match and present a perfect picture as we pace the decks."

I was glad that I had plenty of white suits to wear.

It was a very gay day for me. Mark Twain took me with him when he was invited up to the Captain's quarters for tea, and it was great fun to go on the bridge where passengers are forbidden to wander, and have all the shiny instruments and their uses explained to me. I saw the compass and the wheel and many other things that were so technical that I couldn't even remember their names. Mark Twain "allowed" it was "a mite bigger than the boats he had piloted," but he had no doubt he could do a pretty good job of it just the same, and after all, "the ocean is a simple thing to navigate compared to a treacherous river!"

Perhaps the ocean heard him and made up its mind to show that its navigation wasn't so simple after all, for that night the danger that is always lurking at sea reared its ugly head. The *S. S. Minnetonka* had an accident.

I had gone to sleep lulled by the blasts of the foghorn. About four o'clock the fog deepened, and despite the warning blasts of the horn, a fishing schooner ran into the *S. S. Minnetonka,* knocking a great hole in the starboard side. The Captain ordered all lifeboats down, as it was impossible for him to ascertain the full extent of the damage at once.

For a few minutes there was wild confusion. People rushed up on deck in all stages of dress and undress. A great many appeared in night attire, with a hastily snatched coat or bathrobe around their shoulders.

Mother, who had been awakened by the crash and heard the lifeboat order, began going down in the trunk for heavy clothes in case we had to go out in the little boats. As I was sound asleep and she didn't want to upset me until it was absolutely necessary, she let me slumber on serenely and watched the excitement on deck from the stateroom window.

People were milling around in a state of wildest confusion until it was discovered that the hole in the ship's side was above the water line. Although the plates were badly damaged, there was no immediate danger since, fortunately, there was a very calm sea. The lifeboat order was countermanded and the good news circulated around.

Just as the panic was subsiding and people were beginning to go back to their cabins, the fog lifted and showed the schooner with her bow completely gone. There was only time for a glimpse of the disabled ship before the fog closed in again.

The Captain of the *S. S. Minnetonka* sent down two lifeboats to see if they could pick up anyone or be of any assistance to the boat, but though the lifeboats cruised around for several hours, there was never any sign of the schooner or of its crew. Finally it was decided that it must have slipped back into the fog and that probably it would be able to patch itself up, as the sea was so calm, and get back to the French Coast, or find the fleet of which it was probably a part. At any rate, we had done all we could.

Mark Twain had also slept through the crash. He and I were about the only ones on the entire ship who had. Directly after, Mark Twain's secretary reported to him, and he hurriedly put on a white Turkish toweling dressing robe over his pink pajamas and went up on deck.

This was the same dressing gown that had created a wild sensation at the sedate and exclusive Brown's Hotel in London when he had walked across the courts clad in its snowy splendor to the baths, as was the custom. Everyone who had a room overlooking the court had peered out of their windows to watch him cross, and the dressing gown had been written up in all the London papers.

It still ran true to form. By the time Mark Twain arrived on deck, the worst fright was over. People knew they would not have to put out to sea in tiny boats. The relief was tremendous, and they were just ready to tease Mr. Clemens about the pink pajamas and his Arabian robe.

In the midst of their half-hysterical exclamations, which were greatly amusing to the person at whom they were aimed, came the moment when the fog lifted and revealed the disabled schooner, and everyone, including Mark Twain, rushed to the rail to look at it.

He watched closely the few seconds there was anything to see, then when the fog like a great gray blanket, suddenly dropped again into place, he made his way to my cabin to see how I had come through the disaster.

Mother met him at the door and told him that she hadn't wanted to frighten me so I was still asleep. Mark Twain turned serious and told Mother. "Next time you'd better not be so considerate of Dorothy's feelings. It's better to be frightened than drowned. I know a lot about boats. They can sink in three minutes. If anything happens again when you're at sea, grab Dorothy at once and come up on deck, just as you are. Don't stop for anything. You see, I didn't waste any time."

He pointed to his own attire and then suddenly becoming aware that his weren't exactly the garments for paying a social call, he added a few words about the boat's safety and beat a hasty retreat.

Of course, I knew nothing of all this and probably never would have until we were safely in New York if Mother hadn't forgotten to tell Mark Twain to keep the secret. The next morning when we were taking our daily promenade, I saw men on pulleys over the ship's side, and Mark Twain told me of the mishap the night before and explained that the men were mending the hole, also that we were going very slowly so they could do it more easily. Instead of being frightened or nervous, as Mother had thought I might be, I had the opposite reaction. Now that it was all safely over, I was rather impressed with the importance of having been in an accident at sea.

Mark Twain laughed. "It didn't do you much good to be in it when you slept all through it."

I wouldn't have been quite so carefree if I had known that until the hole was adequately fixed there was still the possibility of danger, for if at any time during the three days it took to mend the hole, there had been a rough sea, the situation would have been very serious. So there was a great deal of nervous tension until the ship's wound was repaired. Some of the passengers slept in their clothes the remainder of the trip. Fortunately, however, the calm seas held, and after crawling along for the three days the repairs took, the S. S. *Minnetonka* continued her voyage.

Mark Twain, who was very kindhearted, immediately interested himself in getting up a statement to the Directors of the Atlantic Transport Line, completely exonerating the S. S. *Minnetonka's* Captain from all blame for the accident. He was the first to sign the document and personally took the trouble to see that everyone else followed his example, which at the first word from him they were only too delighted to do.

I went with him while he got the signatures and so had the opportunity of meeting nearly every one of the passengers. The S. S. *Minnetonka* had only first-class passengers, and instead of steerage, transported animals in the lower decks.

Mark Twain went on a tour of inspection of their quarters and came back very enthusiastic over the way the animals were taken care of. He spent a long time telling me the charms of several fascinating horses that were "belowstairs."

I hadn't gone with him as I had been engrossed in a game of shuffleboard at the time, but when I heard all about the animals, I regretted not having been along. But Mark Twain said, "It's just as well. The air up here is better than down there, and your nose is much too little to put a strain on it."

When I played shuffleboard, or "Horse Billiards," as Mark Twain called it, he would have his chair moved where he could see and "superintend" the play. He would even watch out to see that I put my coat around my shoulders between plays, for which attention I was not as grateful as I should have been. It was such a nuisance putting on and off the coat, and Mark Twain was very meticulous about such things. "So you won't catch cold, dear heart," he would say when I rebelled, and I've no doubt he saved me from many a bout with bronchitis throughout the trip by his thoughtfulness. When I was eliminated from the junior shuffleboard tournament, he gave me his book, *Eve's Diary,* with the inscription:

To Dorothy, with the affectionate regards of the author. Prize for good play in Horse Billiards Tournament. July 10, 1907.

Mark Twain

I was much prouder of this than I would have been of winning the real prize, especially when, with great ceremony, Mark Twain escorted Mother and me to his stateroom and told his secretary to spread out a number of his photographs so that I could choose one for my very own.

There were twenty or more different poses, and it was terribly difficult to decide which one to take. There were head studies, full-length pictures, and three-quarter ones—photographs of him in all his favorite poses that were already familiar to me. They were all splendid and lifelike, for Mark Twain always photographed exceedingly well.

I considered them all for a long time and finally selected a head study.

"Don't you want one in my white suit?" Mark Twain asked. "You've picked out the smallest of them all."

I hesitated. I did, of course, want the larger picture. Anyone would have, but I wanted most of all the one I had chosen.

"I like this the best," I said, clutching it firmly. "It looks just like you do when you talk."

Mark Twain autographed it for me, and then gave me the big picture too and put his signature on that one as well. When I thanked him I said that I thought as long as he was on hand it was better by far to lose a tournament than to win, and the next time I wouldn't even try to get to first place.

Mark Twain's answer to that came quick and sure. "That's a grand idea for shuffleboard, but you'd better not apply it to other things. You might get left if you did and I wouldn't want that to happen to you, Dorothy dear, no matter what game you were playing."

3

Flying Fish and Baked Potatoes

AT FIRST I CALLED HIM "Mr. Twain," then "Mr. Clemens,"
and sometimes very irreverently, "Mark," which lack of ceremony he seemed to enjoy. It wasn't until much later that I
found the name for him that I liked best, "SLC." I discovered
it when I was looking through his books at Tuxedo and found
one in which he had written the date and his initials, SLC,
all run together. I clapped my hands and called out excitedly,
"Mark, I've found my name for you!"

He came over to me and asked. "Well, now, what's it going
to be?"

I showed him the book with the hastily scrawled initials.
"I'm going to call you SLC because it's different, and it can
be my own special name for you."

He thought a minute. "Then that's decided. I think I shall
like it, Dorothy dear, and I will sign my letters to you that
way if you prefer. After all, it's a great deal less trouble than

writing out either Mark Twain or Samuel L. Clemens, and I was never one to make any more effort than I have to!"

So that was settled, and after that each letter I received from him bore the name I had chosen, SLC.

But on the steamer it was still Mr. Twain!

Every morning we would take a walk together just as soon as he came up on deck. We would be constantly interrupted by people who wanted to talk to him, even though he remarked that "a walk isn't much good for a body unless they keep at it."

One very bright day when the ocean was rather rough, I saw a school of small fish which seemed to soar over and below the waves. They weren't like porpoises which dipped into the waves and out. These fish skimmed along, raising themselves into the air in what seemed to me a truly miraculous fashion.

"Do look at those funny fish." I pointed to the spot where they were. We walked toward the rail, and Mark Twain took a brief glance in the line of my extended arm.

"Those are flying fish. My, but you're a lucky child. It isn't often one catches a glimpse of these almost fabulous creatures! They are really prehistoric and once ages ago they were half-bird, half-fish. Gradually they took more and more to the water until they became wholly fish, but they kept their wings for protection so that they could fly away from their enemies, the larger fish, so that all that is left over from the time when they were able to fly long distances are those tiny wings which can still bear their weight and allow them to fly over the water."

"Flying fish!" I was amazed. I had heard of them but had no idea they actually existed. "I thought they only belonged in Arabian Nights!" I finally exclaimed.

"Many of the things in fairy stories had their foundation in actual facts. Even Rip Van Winkle could have been in a state of suspended animation while he slept his twenty years."

"Or the Sleeping Beauty," I added, entranced by the pictures he was evoking. But before I could go on with the subject, he reverted back to the flying fish.

"Can you see their wings?" he asked.

I shook my head. I could see fast-moving objects of a rather hazy and blurred silver-blue that varied in length from ten to twenty inches.

"Then watch closely and after the flight through the air, when the fish approach the crest of a wave, you will see that they momentarily stop the wing movement and slow down enough for you to observe the flapping of their wings."

Now Mark Twain pointed, and I followed the line of his finger and saw the actual movement of the wings–very hazily.

"You're lucky to see them," he repeated. "These fish only appear when the sea is disturbed or very rough. They make great headway against the wind and can fly as fast as ten or fifteen miles an hour, though never more than five hundred feet at a time."

"Goodness! You know a lot about flying fish!" I remarked, considerably impressed by his knowledge of aquatic things.

The little laugh lines in the corner of his eyes crinkled into their creases. "You shouldn't be surprised at anything I know, Dorothy. After all, you can't be over seventy and not know a little about everything!"

"How old are you, Mark?" I asked.

He looked at me quizzically. "Well, the last time I was weighed, I was almost seventy-two," he replied, and I didn't know whether he was joking or not.

In those days, and it wasn't so very long ago, there actually was a "ship's company." The *S. S. Minnetonka* wasn't a *Normandie* or a *Bremen,* where you almost have to have a guide to show you how to find your stateroom. The *S. S. Minnetonka* was small and did not have a large passenger list, so everyone knew everyone else—even Mark Twain. As for me, I had never had so much attention. People who wanted to get to know Mark Twain better decided, since they saw how much I was with him, that I was a good line of approach. If I hadn't been so engrossed in him myself, they might have made some impression, but I was far too interested to want to share even a second of his time. I monopolized him all the daylight hours I could because, as I carefully explained to him, "The other people can talk to you when I've gone to bed. I have to go so early!" I wound up almost in a wail for I did hate to miss a moment of his fascinating society. I had never known anyone who told me so many delightful stories or who treated me so much like a grown-up.

In the dining salon Mark Twain was, of course, seated at the Captain's table. The S. S. *Minnetonka*, like all liners, followed the custom of putting people of prominence at the Captain's table as a tribute. So Mark Twain naturally was placed at the Captain's right. From where I sat I had a splendid view of him and he could easily see me. So lots of smiles and silent messages flew back and forth across the dining room.

Sometimes, when the Captain was busily engaged in conversation with the lady on his left, Mark Twain would sneak away from the table with only a murmured "I forgot something" to his neighbor. Then he would make his way over to where we were sitting, with an expression like a mischievous little boy who knows he has been naughty on his fine face. Quite often at luncheon I would look up to see him standing beside me, with the steward ready with a chair to put next to mine.

"I just thought I'd come along to see what you were doing," he would say, not even looking at the table he had left, although generally by this time someone at it was expressing in pantomime disapproval of his desertion.

Once when he had had only the soup course at his own table, he joined us and ordered some baked potatoes done in a way of which he was especially fond. He had just about finished eating them when the steward from the Captain's table arrived with a plateful of the same dish.

"Captain's compliments, sir. He says they're better at his own table than anywhere else."

Mark Twain accepted the offering and waved his thanks over to the Captain. He then proceeded to dip into the second plate of baked potatoes, and before long it was emptier than the first.

I asked if it really was any better. He winked at me and swore, "they tasted exactly alike," which I considered a very good joke on the Captain.

"Just wait until I take the conceit out of his sails on the baked potato question!"

After he had left his own table for lunch on three successive days to sit with me, one of the passengers who was an artist drew a picture of Buster Brown, the popular comic of the time. Buster, with sprouting wings, was standing by himself in a corner, looking at the following caption:

> RESOLVED: That Mark Twain has deserted the entire ship's company for Dorothy Quick. I wish my name was "Twain!"
> —Buster.

When I heard, the night of the baked-potato episode, that roars of laughter had gone up from the Captain's table, for once I didn't mind having my dinner early and being in bed when all the excitement was going on, for I knew what all the mirth was about—baked potatoes!

4

Mark Twain's Business Manager

ONE DAY TOWARD THE END OF THE VOYAGE, I was standing at the ship's rail trying to see if there were any more flying fish about, when all at once I heard an unknown masculine voice.

"Miss Quick?"

I wheeled around and saw a line of three men. In the center was one of the ship's officers, very smart in white linen with his stripes and gilt buttons. He was flanked on either side by passengers whom I recognized as Mr. Cook and Mr. Ryan.

The officer saluted ostentatiously. "Have I the pleasure of addressing Mark Twain's business manager?" he asked.

I had been a little startled by all this, but when I heard the "Mark Twain's business manager," I giggled a little because I suspected it was one of Mr. Clemens' jokes.

"Oh, no, I'm not. Mr. Twain calls me his business manager sometimes, but I don't think he is serious," I replied.

"Indeed he is," the officer told me. "We just asked him if he would make a speech at the ship's concert and he said, 'I never do anything unless my business manager says I may, so you'll have to ask Dorothy.' "

My heart began to beat so fast that I could feel it thumping against my ribs. Mark Twain had been wonderful to me in giving me his friendship. It did not seem possible that there could be any more gifts for me in his Santa Claus bag, but here was an honor that, like Juliet, I had not dreamed of.

Once again the officer, with a click of his heels and a flash of gilt braid, saluted. "Miss Quick, will you please give permission for Mark Twain to speak at the concert for the benefit of the sailor's fund?"

The eyes of all three men were riveted upon me. I had never felt so important. Literally, I was up in the air, I was so proud. I took a deep breath before I replied.

"Of course. I will be delighted to." The grown-up speech came easily to my lips. I had heard Mother say it often and felt it was just the thing for this occasion, but before they could reply, I said the thing that was uppermost in my mind. "I'm just crazy to hear him speak, myself!"

Let it be written down to their credit that these three men didn't smile over a little girl's naïveté. Instead, they thanked me as seriously, as though I had been as old as Mark Twain himself. Then they saluted and turned on their heels and walked toward the bow, where Mark Twain had been standing watching the procedure.

As soon as I caught sight of his familiar figure, I ran to him and began to tell him how glad I was he was going to speak, and how excited I was that I had been asked to give my permission.

"Imagine asking me if you could speak!" I exclaimed.

"Why not?" Mark Twain spoke quite seriously. "You're my business manager for this trip, anyway, and I'm strongly considering giving you the job for life." He watched me as I stared at him, my eyes wide with incredulity.

"I couldn't say a word unless you consented. Only, next time don't do it so quickly. You should have held out on them a little. It's more fun if you keep people in suspense a while and makes them feel happier when you finally give in."

The night of the concert no one on the ship was in such a flutter as I, for in large letters on the program was printed:

MARK TWAIN
BY COURTESY OF MISS DOROTHY QUICK

Imagine my pride and delight! I read it over and over, and all the time Mark Twain was speaking the magic words were superimposed on his white-clad figure.

He talked about the improvement of the conditions of the adult blind and repeated the story he had told in *A Tramp Abroad* of having been caught with a companion in Berlin in the dark for an hour or more, enlarging on his horror at not being able to see for even so short a time.

There never was a speaker who could paint more realistic word pictures or grip his audience as Mark Twain did. With a few sentences he held all the people who were crowded into the ship's lounge literally breathless. With the magic of his words he wove a spell around them until they lived the situation just as he had done, and when he finished by saying that he would devote much of his life to the subject of aiding the blind, the passengers arose in a body and promised their aid in anything he undertook.

There was never a person kinder and more considerate of others than Mark Twain. He had a great sense of fair play and an inordinate amount of pity for those less fortunate than himself, so that it was particularly like him to take every opportunity that presented itself to help a cause in which he was interested.

Shortly before this trip he had met Helen Keller and had been much impressed with the wonderful things her teacher had done to improve her condition. He had told me about her and how the teacher had made the blind deaf-mute "see" and "hear" by the aid of finger-talking. Whenever he could, he put in a good word for the aid of the blind.

His speeches were always amusing and clever and never failed to provide laughter and mirth from his audience. He could make them laugh whenever he wanted to, and because of the very good humor into which he put them, he could drive home the point he wished to make—and there always was a point. He would dress it up in giggles and laughs, but its sharpness was still there. He never made a speech that did not have a serious background, a message behind its mirth.

That night at the concert was no exception. People forgot the things that at the time had made them howl with glee, but they did not forget his appeal for the blind. That was something they always remembered.

I had more than that to remember. I had the great and, to me, the glorious fact that he had paid me the honor of making the speech "By courtesy of Miss Dorothy Quick," and it gave each word he uttered an added importance in my mind.

That night I felt I had reached a pinnacle that I might never climb again, and I relished each second to its utmost capacity.

The concert program read:

PROGRAM

Atlantic Transport Line
S. S. *Minnetonka*

Program
of
Evening of Humor and Song
To be held in the Salon en route
Saturday, July 20th, 1907
To commence at 8:30 P. M.

Master of Ceremonies _____Mr. Willet F. Cook

Program

1. Introductory remarks _____Mr. Sydney H. Carragan
2. Song, with violin obligato ___Miss Hurst and Miss Hyde
3. Recitation _____Roderick Dhu and Fitz James
4. Mark Twain (By courtesy of Miss Dorothy Quick)
5. Song _____Mr. H. W. Truman
    Mrs. W. E. Truman, Accompanist
6. Collection
7. Fog Horn Quartette_____ Messrs. W. E. & H. W. Truman,
    C. Weddle & E. F. Trevers
8. Presentation of prizes to the winners of the
    Sports Contest by Mr. F. S. Goodman
9. America and God Save the King_____by 120 Sea Gulls
    — GOOD NIGHT —

5

Home-Coming Is Not Leave-Taking

THE FIRST TIME I ever had my picture taken with Mark Twain was one lovely sunshiny day when we were halfway across the Atlantic Ocean. One of the passengers snapped it while I was sitting on the end of his steamer chair.

Such a funny, serious little girl, looking straight ahead at the camera from under heavy eyelashes and brows!

My only concessions to his love of white that day were my stockings, hair ribbons, and a white veil which tied down my tam-o-shanter. Otherwise I wore a blue sailor suit and a dark blue coat. Mark Twain, too, bowing to the chill in the air, wore gray and as a special favor to the photographer, turned back the peak of his gray cap so that it wouldn't overshadow his face. The result was that, except for the white hair and moustache, he might have passed for a Heidelberg student, especially since his bowl pipe added to the illusion.

I had my arm around his knee and looked very stern, as though I were guarding him from all intruders. Evidently the picture-taking was a very serious business, for Mark Twain himself looked grave.

Captain Layland, who often asked us up to his quarters, sometimes returned our visits by coming down to walk with us on deck. Some pictures were taken of the three of us. If they had been posed according to height, we would have looked like steps, since the Captain was exceedingly tall, Mr. Clemens was about medium, and I was quite a lot shorter. But there was no picture like that for, with true gallantry, the Captain and Mr. Clemens, as I was now calling him, put me between them, each holding one of my hands. Several pictures were taken, and when the passengers saw what was going on, they ran for their kodaks and asked if they, too, might snap us—and Mr. Clemens obligingly said "Yes."

As soon as the pictures were developed by the ship's photographer, everyone came rushing to Mark Twain with requests that he autograph them. Even I was asked to append my signature, and added a scrawly "Dorothy Quick" below Mr. Clemens' "Mark Twain." I felt very important as I did so, although I knew it was wanted only because of my association with him.

All this, however, was nothing to the orgy of picture-taking that occurred when the S. S. Minnetonka arrived in New York.

I had expected I would be very sad as we steamed up the harbor, for I thought it would mean the end of a friendship that had grown to be very precious. I was too young to appreciate what so close a companionship with a man like Mark Twain meant; but I did know I should miss a grand playmate and storyteller, and I was sure that it would be difficult to settle down to everyday life after the glamorous time I had been having.

However, I didn't need to be worried about being blue as

we sailed up the harbor. I didn't have time to feel any emotion but interest, for a bevy of reporters boarded the ship at Quarantine armed with notebooks and cameras, all ready to be focused on Mark Twain.

He met them and answered all their questions in his most agreeable manner, but when they wanted to take his picture he refused unless I could be photographed with him. So his secretary was sent to ask Mother if it would be all right, and when she consented the photographing began in earnest.

I had never looked into so many cameras at once. They all clicked merrily, with the result that there was not a paper in New York the next day that didn't carry a photograph of "Mark Twain and Dorothy Quick."

After they had finished photographing, they asked Mr. Clemens more questions and he elaborated on what a good time he had had in England and how he had swapped jokes with the King. But he wouldn't tell them the jokes or give away any of the good stories for which he was famous because, as he said, "I get paid for those."

When they asked him about the accident, he replied, "Of the collision I saw nothing. I was disappointed because I felt I should have been notified beforehand." This brought a smile to the reporters' faces and made me laugh outright.

Then they asked him what he knew about the Ascot Cup and the Dublin jewels, both of which had been stolen while he was in England. He replied, "As to the Ascot Cup, I don't mind taking you all into my confidence. It's on board this ship and I expect to get it ashore if I have any luck and use diplomacy. As to my lifting the Dublin jewels, the idea is absurd. Wasn't the safe left? Can it be thought for a moment that I would take the jewels without taking the safe?"

This brought forth more gales of merriment and made the

reporters forget to ask questions for a few minutes. Then they returned to the charge and tried to coax a story from him, but he remained firm.

"The best story I heard in England is not one that I am going to tell now. I get thirty cents a word for stories and my rate is the same for jokes—no rebate."

Then someone asked if anyone else ever succeeded in getting a joke through the English.

Mark Twain said, "Now, that does not suggest a broad view of the situation. Humor isn't a thing of race or nationality. So much depends upon the environment of a joke. To be good it must absorb its setting. The American joke does this—so does the English. Believe it or not, I have met English folks that were funny."

A very diplomatic reply.

I've often wondered if Mark Twain in this speech wasn't the originator of the "Believe it or not" phrase that Robert Ripley has since made famous.

After a while even the reporters became satisfied, and as the boat nosed into the dock they rushed off to get their articles to press.

When the papers came out, the headlines were varied. "MARK TWAIN HOME—CAPTIVE OF LITTLE GIRL" was the one they used most. And what thrilled me most of all, after seeing the pictures, were the long paragraphs about me, which even told how Mark Twain had refused to speak at the concert without my permission.

One writer called me "the Fidgety Miss Quick," which adjective was annoying but deserved, for I never was good at sitting still and they had spent hours over those pictures.

One paper amused me greatly, for it went into great detail about the collision and said that when it took place Mark

Twain put on his Oxford gown and rushed to my cabin and carried me up on deck. This, while far from the truth, certainly made a dramatic story.

The reporters had no sooner left us on the sun deck than the admiring fellow passengers clustered about Mr. Clemens with last-minute requests for autographs and farewells, so that Mr. Clemens was kept busy and I didn't have time even to think about the coming separation.

Mr. Clemens and I descended the gangplank together, and I was immediately introduced to another secretary of his who had come to meet the boat and who said she was very glad to know me as she'd heard a great deal about "Dorothy." This puzzled me for I didn't see how someone in New York could have known so much about what happened on the *S. S. Minnetonka.* It was not until I was on my way home that the riddle was solved for me by my Mother. She explained about the wireless messages and said that Mark Twain had undoubtedly wired ahead about his little friend at the same time he had sent news of the accident. Wireless was not the ordinary matter-of-fact thing it is now, and although I had been abroad several times in my short life, I had never had any experience with wireless messages before.

On the pier Mark Twain introduced me to his publishers, who had come to greet him on his return to America. They were feeling even more proud of the honors that had been heaped upon him than he was himself. I met Frederick A. Duneka of Harper and Brothers, and David Munro of the *North American Review.* They were both exceedingly nice to me, but before long they began to discuss business with their own special celebrity and I skipped over to where my family was.

When the customs were finished, I asked Mother to go with

me while I said good-by to Mr. Clemens, As we started, the depression which I had expected to feel coming up the harbor descended upon me. I was a very intense child, strong in my likes and dislikes. Loving few outside of my family, I had given my heart to Mr. Clemens in a combination of hero worship and the deep affection that it is only possible for a child to hold.

Halfway across from *Q* to *C* we met Mr. Clemens, who was coming in search of me. Before I could say good-bye, Mr. Clemens asked Mother if she would let me come and visit him at his home in Tuxedo Park. Mother nodded, and then he turned and asked me if I would come.

The black cloud lifted. This was not the end. Our friendship hadn't been only a shipboard acquaintance which would fade away as ships do on a distant horizon. I would see him again. The delightful stories and games would continue. He wanted me to visit him! But could I go? I had never been away from Mother a single night in my life—never separated from her. I didn't see how I ever could be.

The seconds passed while Mother and Mr. Clemens waited anxiously. They knew the struggle that was going on in my mind. Mother looked at me and nodded her head for me to say "yes."

That won the day. I knew that I would like to be with Mark Twain, and I was happy that he wanted me to come and that Mother wanted me to go. I clutched Mother's hand firmly to give me courage and said, greatly to the relief of my listeners, "I'd just love to come."

There was a short discussion of convenient times for the visit. Then Mr. Clemens said he would write and kissed me good-by, telling me not to forget him, which was so absurd that we both laughed.

6

An Invitation from Mark Twain

I WENT IMMEDIATELY TO Plainfield, New Jersey, with my family and expected to settle down once more to an ordinary existence. But it wasn't to be so. I was like the girl in the fairy story who stole a drop of the elves' ointment and put it on her eyes and ever afterward saw everything as the elves saw it—transcendently beautiful. I had been touched with magic ointment, too, and things were never quite the same afterward.

The very next morning before we had even had time to unpack, word was brought that a feature writer from the *New York American* was waiting to interview "Miss Quick."

So down I went with Mother and met the lady who asked me innumerable questions, most of which I didn't answer. I adored Mark Twain and was glad he liked me, but I didn't see why the world should want to hear about it.

But I did tell Miss Anna Steese Richardson how the love of books had drawn us together. "You see," I said, "when we first met, he learned that I had read every one of his books before I ever met him. I think he liked that. All people who write books like to know you read them. After that he made me do most of the talking. Since Mark Twain wrote *Huckleberry Finn*, lots and lots of books have been written for children that he has never read. So I told him all about those books and he was interested."

I did enjoy reading the article when it came out in the Sunday magazine section of the *New York American*. It was called "Me and Mark Twain," with the caption, "The Little New York girl who conquered the great humorist on his ocean trip tells her own story of that romantic incident."

Of course, I'd hardly talked at all and had spent most of my time wishing Miss Richardson would go so I could play with my friends, but according to the article I had been very confiding. Several of the pictures were reproduced, but what I liked best was a sketch of Mark Twain and me seated on the bow of an ocean liner—I very comfortably ensconced on his lap, waving an American flag.

Mr. Clemens thought that this was the best of all the write-ups and that it had decidedly given him a new idea. He had never traveled on the bow of a ship, but he said he thought he would like to try it if I would go along.

There were still further excitements in store for me, for one morning the mailman brought an invitation from Mark Twain.

TUXEDO PARK
NEW YORK

DOROTHY DEAR,
Will you come and make me a visit? Do you think your Mother could spare you a week? Will you come? If you can't come for a whole week, will you come for half a week? But I hope you can make it a whole one. It is beautiful here—lakes, woods, hills

38

and everything! Yes, quite beautiful and satisfactory but I miss you all the same. I hope you will remember me most kindly to your Mother and to your Grandfather and Grandmother and that you will allow me to keep my place as your ancient and affectionate friend.

S. L. CLEMENS

At the same time he wrote Mother and explained that his secretary was quite able to take care of me as she had been a governess and was forty-three years old—and that he would have her come for me and bring me home.

Now I was in a great state—torn between my desire to go and my fear of leaving Mother. A compromise was finally effected, and I wrote back accepting—not for a whole week, for that seemed a little too long to be away from home, but for the "inside of a week." The letters flew back and forth concerning arrangements for the visit, and finally Mother decided to motor me up.

Mr. Clemens wanted to know the very hour we would arrive, and a bustle of preparation went on in Plainfield and Tuxedo.

Finally my bags were packed and everything was ready for the journey. With the sun shining brightly as an omen of the golden days to come, I started forth on my first visit to Mark Twain.

7

Tuxedo Park

TUXEDO PARK! That exclusive colony in the Ramapo Hills where a goodly part of New York's four hundred tucked themselves away. To have a house there in those days was to bear the stamp of social success. The Park was the retreat of aristocracy. Here, surrounded by walls through which lodge gates were the only means of entrance, they were firmly entrenched. No one could pass the gates unless they were either a resident or visiting someone who was, in which case they had to be vouched for by the person they were going to see.

Mr. Clemens in his letters had asked by what road we were coming, and I had told him that we would arrive at the main entrance about four o'clock. So he had given instructions that we were to be passed through immediately.

We weren't as prompt in arriving as we had anticipated. To begin with, we started later than we had planned and then instead of coming on the road which would have brought us to the main entrance, we missed it while making a detour and finally arrived at one of the smaller lodges about a quarter of five.

There was an iron grille barring our way. A gatekeeper came out, and we explained we were going to visit Mr. S. L. Clemens and that as we were late we'd appreciate it if he'd let us go straight through.

Not at all! That we were late meant nothing against the rules and regulations. The gatekeeper was very sorry, but as he had no instructions about us, we must wait while he telephoned Mr. Clemens' house. We explained that Mr. Clemens had said he would give instructions to admit us, but that made no impression. He still must telephone. In those days telephones were not the simple easy things they are now; to telephone from the lodge to the house Mr. Clemens had rented for the season took time. However, there was nothing for us to do but exercise patience. After what seemed an interminably long wait the man returned and told us what we already knew—that we were expected!

Presently he swung open the heavy gates, and we passed through and at last were on our way. The car, making a great deal of noise as it negotiated the hilly roads, announced our arrival long before we drove up in front of the house.

A great many of the Tuxedo houses are set almost on the road. As there was a very small amount of traffic inside the Park and the roads were all private to the residents, there was not the necessity for having the houses surrounded by grounds. All of the Park was a picturesque landscape.

Mr. Clemens' house had its entrance very near the road, requiring only a short walk up to the front door. On the other side the house was built over a cliff-like formation so that the upstairs windows looked out over the tops of the trees toward the lake and the mountains which made an incomparable vista.

There was a porch on one end of the house that extended around to the lakeside, and above it on the second floor was a round porch opening from Mr. Clemens' own room, all of which commanded the same magnificent view of the lake and hills. Below both of these porches was still another on the garden level to which a flight of brick stairs led down. The house was really built on three levels on the garden side like a tiered cake.

At the time of our arrival, however, I saw nothing but Mark Twain's white-clad figure standing before the front door. He was running his fingers through his hair as he often did when excited and alternately waving a welcome. I jumped out of the car and ran to him, and his joy at seeing me was so mixed up with his anger at the gatekeeper for holding us up that it was difficult to distinguish which was which.

One second he was saying how glad he was that I had come; the next, calling instructions to his secretary who had just gotten the main lodge on the phone, telling her to be sure they understood that such a thing must never happen again. When they had been given instructions at one lodge, it should be automatically passed on to all the others.

"I've got no use for stupid people and such ridiculous red tape," he exclaimed testily. "The idea! Keeping you waiting when I am in such a hurry!"

Then, the lodge keeper having been scolded to his satisfaction, he dismissed the matter entirely and devoted his attention to welcoming us and apologizing for the stupidity which had delayed our arrival. I had hardly had time to get my breath when he said, "You tardy little rascal! I thought you'd never come! I've got a jigger waiting and we've been due at tea for half an hour."

For the first time I was conscious of a chug-chugging noise which was more noticeable now that the engine of our own car had stopped. I looked around and saw standing in the road a small black car.

"Is that a jigger?" I asked, looking toward it.

Mr. Clemens nodded. "That's the Tuxedo name for the taxis that run around inside the Park and they're well-named, too. Wait until you see how it jiggles you along! And speaking of that, we must hurry!"

Mother and Mr. Clemens' secretary whisked me upstairs to change my dress and down again to the accompaniment of Mr. Clemens' calling "Hurry!" up the stairs every few minutes.

I didn't have time to notice the interior of the house or even think about good-by to Mother. Before I knew what was happening, I was in the jigger with Mr. Clemens, and it was living up to its reputation by bouncing along. At the time I thought it funny that he hurried me so. I didn't realize that his anxiety to get started was part of a well-laid plan—one more evidence of his knowledge of human nature. He didn't want me to be homesick and he knew once the break had been made there would be clear sailing. Thus he hadn't given me a chance to get upset over any good-bys, although he had been quite thoughtful in leaving explanations of his haste with his secretary for my Mother.

All the way to the tea he kept me busy exclaiming over the scenery.

"Tuxedo is one of the loveliest places this part of America can boast about," he told me.

I remembered that when he invited me to visit him, he had written, "It's beautiful here, lakes, woods, hills and everything,"and now that I was seeing it for myself, I could understand his enthusiasm. It *was* beautiful—a symphony in green with the trees dominating everything as they stood etched against the clear blue of the sky.

We passed many magnificent estates—some close to the road, as Mr. Clemens' house was, others set far back so one could only catch a glimpse of their elegance through the trees. Mr. Clemens told me who lived in each place as we passed, and whether he liked the house or not. He had very strong likes and dislikes and never had the least hesitancy about expressing them.

After a ride which seemed exceedingly short, but in reality was several miles long, we turned into a driveway that wound its way upward to a huge shingled house that stood on a high knoll. There were any number of private cars and jiggers clustered around the porte-cochere and Mr. Clemens said, "See all the people that have come to meet you, Dorothy."

I giggled. I knew perfectly well whom they had come to meet, and he knew it just as well as I did.

"They have come to see you!" I exclaimed.

"I can't fool you, can I?" he chuckled, as he helped me out of the jigger.

We walked across a large porch, hand in hand. A butler swung open the door and escorted us to the living room with great ceremony. As we stood on the threshold of an imposing oak-paneled room and looked at what seemed like hundreds of people who were all engrossed in conversation, laughing and chattering, I felt a sudden panic. Although all my life I had been more with older people than with children of my own age, they had been people I knew. Here I was only a little girl in the midst of strange grown-ups, and I was frightened. I clung tightly to Mr. Clemens' hand.

"They're making more noise than a Sunday School picnic,"

44

he whispered in my ear while we waited for the butler to announce us. Whether he had sensed my nervousness or not, the remark put me at ease. All at once I wasn't a lonely little girl surrounded by strangers; I was a person sharing a secret with a friend, and nothing else mattered.

"Mr. Clemens." The butler's voice, swollen with the importance of his announcement, carried into the room and produced an immediate result. The conversation ceased. There was instantaneously the silence that is the sincerest tribute to greatness. Then the hostess, a tall and stately *grande dame* with a manner as dignified and imposing as her house, moved toward us.

If a king had arrived, he could not have attracted more deference and attention than Mr. Clemens did that August afternoon. Tuxedo had never before had such a celebrity in its midst, and Mark Twain was loved for himself as well as for his fame. The hostess had hardly exchanged greetings with us than Mr. Clemens was surrounded by a circle of admirers who literally hung on every word he said, and he enjoyed it. The man whom his intimates called the "King" was not adverse to admiration. In fact, he thrived upon it.

"I like being the center of attraction. It's very pleasing, and no trouble!" he told me many months later, but that day in Tuxedo I almost knew it without words. I could tell that Mr. Clemens was enjoying himself by the sparkle in his eyes and the alertness of his gestures, despite his poker face which never betrayed his feelings. I have seen him have a whole roomful of people convulsed over the things he was saying, with a perfectly straight face and not even a curve of his lips to betray that he was enjoying the joke as much as they were.

As I watched him being swept farther from me by the adoring throngs, the lonely feeling took possession of me again.

In my heart I almost wished Mark Twain was not quite so popular. If he weren't, I would not be entirely alone with a lot of people I had never seen before who were already asking me questions. "How long have you known Mark Twain? Is he fascinating to visit? Does he always tell funny stories?" were only a few of them.

My hostess rescued me, and taking my hand, led me toward the dining room. I could see a long table covered with fine linen and shining silver which stood out against great masses of delphiniums and roses. There was only time for a glimpse before I heard Mr. Clemens' voice asking, "Where's Dorothy?" His reached me over all the other voices in the room, and, because I knew he hadn't forgotten me, the words did away with the lonely feeling forever.

In a few seconds he made his way through the crowd to where I was.

"I almost lost you," he said. "We won't let that happen again."

"I was just going to get some ice cream for Dorothy," the hostess told him.

Mr. Clemens thought that was a splendid idea. We went in to the lovely table together, and pretty soon we were both eating ice cream, surrounded by the inevitable circle that Mr. Clemens always attracted.

The rest of the time passed very quickly. If I heard once the story of my meeting with Mr. Clemens, I must have heard it fifty times. Everyone wanted to know about me, and Mr. Clemens delighted in answering the questions that I had found overwhelming. His favorite way of introducing me was "This is Dorothy, who knows more about my books than I do." This never failed to bring a ripple of laughter from whomever it was addressed to, and usually resulted in an endeavor to ascertain if I could live up to my reputation.

Because they saw that it pleased Mr. Clemens, everyone was terribly nice to me. On the way home I said I felt a little embarrassed at the fuss they made over me. Mr. Clemens patted me on the shoulder and said, "Don't let that worry you. If anyone sets you on a bed of roses, don't ask questions, just enjoy it—only be sure first there aren't any thorns. Not that anyone would ever put thorns out for you, Dorothy, but just the same it wouldn't be well at any time to eat more than two plates of ice cream. For ice cream, while soft as roses and very pleasing to the palate can become quite a prickly thorn in your insides if it happens to disagree with you."

This was another one of his little jokes at my expense for I had been too excited at the party to even finish my one plate of ice cream, let alone think of two!

Nevertheless, we had a good laugh over it on the way home, and I decided that going to tea with Mark Twain and basking in the reflection of his glory was about the most exciting thing I had ever done.

8

After Dinner, the Orchestrelle

WHEN WE GOT HOME from the tea, it was almost dinnertime, so there was still no opportunity to explore the interior of the house. However, it didn't take very long to get a general idea of the rooms on the ground floor.

There was a large spacious hall with a curving stairway on the right, gently sloping upward. On the left of the hall, framed by an open arched doorway were steps which led down into the living room.

This room was charming—a typical country-house room, very light, with a breeze always sweeping through from the many windows and the door leading to the side porch. The furniture was chintz covered and comfortable. There were lots of little tables about, ever ready to receive the ashes from Mr. Clemens' big black cigars. But the thing that stood out most in the long room was the orchestrelle. Mr. Clemens showed it to me proudly and said that we would have music after dinner. "Beautiful music, Dorothy, recorded by the world's greatest artists."

After Dinner, the Orchestrelle

I expect I must have looked a little bewildered, for he went
on to explain that the organ worked on the same principal as
a player piano. I was on familiar ground at once for I knew
all about playing rolls on a piano. It had never occurred to me
that the same principle could be used for an organ. I was full
of curiosity and eager to have some music at once to see how
it worked, but just then Claude, the butler, announced that
dinner was served. Mr. Clemens with much ceremony offered
me his arm, and we proceeded to the table in great state, with
Mr. Clemens' secretary humming a little march as we went.

The dining room was very gracious and cheerful, with white
woodwork, old mahogany, and shining silver. It was ably pre-
sided over by Claude who was, without doubt, the perfect
butler. Many is the dish that he coaxed Mr. Clemens to sample
which, without his solicitation, would have been untouched,
for Mr. Clemens was never very much of an eater and had an
appetite that had to be teased along. He believed in eating
when one felt hungry, and he was very apt to become involved
in a discussion or a talk which interested him so much that
he forgot to be hungry. I am sure if it hadn't been for Claude's
gentle insistence, Mr. Clemens would have gone supperless
to bed very often!

However, Claude took great care that this didn't happen.
If Mr. Clemens was so busy telling one of his inimitable stories
that he merely waved the food aside, Claude would always
put the choicest morsel on his plate anyway and see that the
plate remained until its contents had been enjoyed.

Claude had been in the Clemens household for years and
was devoted to his employer. This devotion was appreciated
by Mr. Clemens, who took a great interest in any member of
his household and was very attached to those of them who had
been with him a long time. Katy Leary, who had grown old

49

in his service, had a particularly warm place in his heart. In fact, he looked on her more as a friend than as a servant.

Dinner was simple and delicious. The menus in the Clemens household were well calculated to be strength-giving as well as tempting. But, truly, the food could have been ambrosial or the very opposite variety, for Mr. Clemens was so interesting and amusing that one quite forgot what one was eating, while listening to him talk.

It made no difference whether there was a great congregation assembled to hear his words or only his secretary and a a little girl; the priceless flow of his humor was unchecked, especially during meals. There seemed to be something about the mere fact of being seated at a table that inspired him to talk. Not that he was ever given to being silent, but at other times he was very intense on whatever he happened to be doing—whether it was work or play. At mealtimes there was nothing to distract him, for, as I have said, food to him was always most unimportant.

At luncheon, I was soon to discover, he never made any attempt to eat at all unless some dish of which he happened to be especially fond was served. When this occurred, he would sit down in his chair and enjoy it; otherwise he would prowl around the table, delivering a monologue or asking everyone their opinion of a subject in which he was interested. When they had all finished, he would state his own views and if anyone had given expression to a different opinion, he would soon wear down that person's argument until not a single leg was left to stand on. This gave him a great deal of pleasure. Somehow he always managed to be in the right. I didn't quite see why it always worked out that way until once after a long, heated discussion in which he had come off victor, he winked at me slowly and deliberately, and whispered, "You notice I always draw them out before I say what *I* think. There's never any use taking chances when you want to come out on top." After that I understood perfectly.

Other times he would draw his chair away from its place at the table and sit down, crossing his legs. Then he would bring out a book from under his arm, or from one of his capacious pockets, and say, "I thought I'd read this to you today." Sometimes it would be one of his own books that he would select to read aloud! other times it would be something he had found which had appealed to him so much that he wanted to share it. But in either case it would be fascinating to hear.

At this, my first dinner in Mr. Clemens' house, there were no arguments or reading. Instead, we discussed the tea we had been to that afternoon, and Mr. Clemens remarked that he thought "Teas were very overrated things. You rarely get anything to eat at them and you seldom hear a body's name."

"Except yours!" I said.

He laughed, pleased at the implied compliment, and finally said that though teas were undoubtedly more trouble than they were worth. Still, he allowed, no one could deny that if one wanted to see and be seen, a tea was the place for it.

After dinner we went back to the living room, and my curiosity over the orchestrelle was fully satisfied, for Mr. Clemens had roll after roll played for us. I chose the couch as my front-row seat for the concert. Mr. Clemens sat in one of the large over-stuffed chairs, completely relaxed, his head resting against its back. He would take long, luxurious draws from his big cigar, and then exhale the smoke lingeringly, as though he were loath to lose its fragrance.

All the time the wonderful music came flowing out into the room. At first it was like the gentle, peaceful waves that caress the beach; then, as the crescendo mounted, they became great breakers that pounded on the feelings, until one felt that they were caught up by the melody and swept away into far, unknown lands wherein there was only beauty. That is the way Mr. Clemens later described it to me, and it was truly so.

Mr. Clemens was never happier than when he was listening to the orchestrelle, and he would sometimes have it played for him for several hours at a time—no mean task, as the foot pedals had to be pumped continuously while it was being played.

Mr. Clemens would lie back in his chair, blowing smoke toward the ceiling, completely lost in the melody. Music, undoubtedly , was one of the joys of his life.

"I like Bach," he said. "There is something transcendently great in those beautiful chords."

There was. But I have often thought that the ideas that were born in Mr. Clemens' mind as he listened were equally great, and when he gave them to the world, they were fully as much appreciated.

After the music, a card table was set up and a pile of games brought out. Mr. Clemens had ordered a large variety in anticipation of my visit. From among them we picked out parcheesi, and Mr. Clemens told me that it was a very ancient game, almost as old as chess, and that the Indian princes all had their parcheesi boards on tables specially made for them, some inlaid with semi-precious stones. This transformed the commonplace game for me into something out of the past and gave it a glamor and excitement it had never had before. So I promptly christened it, "The Indian Game," and Mr. Clemens said he didn't know whether he'd be a rajah or a prince, but he thought he'd be a rajah.

"A Rajah is better than a Prince because you couldn't mistake what Rajah meant, and Prince has become so much associated with dogs!" He added, "I wouldn't mind being a gay young dog, but I would object most certainly to being considered the household variety, and as you can't rely on people's judgment, it is better to be plain about your meanings!"

The hours flew by until all of a sudden Mr. Clemens discovered it was long past my bedtime, and the game was reluctantly broken off. I had finished the eventual winner out of the series of games.

"That's only because you've just come, Dorothy," Mr. Clemens explained, "and I'm being polite. It's an effort and I don't think I could keep it up very long. So you might just as well make up your mind to losing after this; but, of course, I'll let you win now and then, just because you are a good little girl and I think virtue should always be rewarded. It so often isn't, that I feel whenever one can do something about it one ought to. One should always set a good example, when it's no trouble."

Catherine, the maid who was looking after me, was rung for, and soon a little procession started up the stairs. The second floor was equally as spacious as the first. Mr. Clemens' room was a large one over the dining room, and the round porch I spoke of before opened out from it. My room was down the hall to the left and was on the corner; in the front there were windows from which one could look down over the garden and the lake.

Mr. Clemens came in to see that everything was in order and sent his secretary off for a bowl of fruit, in case I should be hungry. When everything had been arranged according to his satisfaction, he told me once more how glad he was that I had come, and the warmth of his words lingered in my heart long after he had said goodnight and gone away.

In fact, I could hear them echoing in my ears as Catherine

tucked me in bed and turned out the light. They were so real, so whole-hearted, that I dropped off to sleep with their warmth still holding me. I hadn't time to be homesick. I hadn't time for anything but the joyous remembrance of the first day of my visit with Mark Twain.

9

We Eat Plums and Take Pictures at Tuxedo Park

THE SUNLIGHT STREAMING in my window woke me up, and I looked at the clock, dismayed upon finding it was after ten. I didn't want to miss any of Mr. Clemens' society, and I didn't yet know that unless there was some special reason, he very rarely appeared in the morning.

"I never get up unless I have to," he told me once. "And I never go to bed if there's anything to do as long as I stay up." He would play billiards on and on into the night until his partners were exhausted, whereas he, himself, would be still as fresh as when he had started the first game. Mr. Clemens had an enormous zest for whatever he was doing and always threw his whole self into it.

I popped out of bed and rang the bell. Presently, Catherine appeared, bringing with her a message from Mr. Clemens saying that he hoped I'd had a good night and would enjoy my breakfast and he would see me downstairs about eleven-thirty.

I had no idea that this was a special honor, but I soon learned.

Claude, whom I met on my way downstairs, told me where I would find my host. When I ran out to the porch, there was Mr. Clemens waiting for me. He greeted me enthusiastically and then stood back and regarded me with a quizzical expression.

"You're a little thing to get a body up so early, especially anyone as lazy as I am. It's to celebrate your arrival that I'm downstairs, because ordinarily I don't come down in the forenoon." And then he went on to explain that he devoted the mornings to his work.

"It has got to be done and that seems the best time, dear heart."

I began to feel guilty at keeping him away from his work, for even one morning, but he didn't give me time to do more than voice my feelings. Brushing it aside as of no consequence, he took me down the steps into the garden.

The garden was at a lower level than the road, so that it was really a sunken one. It was long and narrow and at the far end was a round bed of nasturtiums; there were flaming orange shades that diminished into pale yellow—a circle of color that caught my attention immediately.

I oh-ed and ah-ed over them, as the bright colors appealed to me even more than the lovely view of the lake or the rose beds.

Mr. Clemens suggested that I pick a bunch of nasturtiums, which I was only too happy to do. Then we took the flowers in and gave them to Claude who fixed them in a silver bowl on the buffet, so we had the gay colors inside the house as well as in the garden.

On our way through the dining room, we discovered a

large dish of plums. Despite my recent breakfast, I looked at them longingly, and Mr. Clemens, who had a sixth sense when it came to other peoples' minds, asked if I wouldn't like one. I said, "Yes," and he allowed he "could do away with one too." We each selected one of the luscious plums and retired to the round porch which overhung the cliff, so we could eat them without danger of the juice falling on our clothes.

I had remembered Mr. Clemens fondness for white, and my wardrobe consisted almost entirely of it, with plenty of bright red hair-ribbons to satisfy my own sense of color.

The next few minutes anyone who had arrived would have been greeted by the sight of the great humorist and a little girl leaning over the porch rail eating plums! It must have been an amusing sight, and I do wish someone could have happened along and snapped our picture. It was a picture that could have been taken several times a day during my Tuxedo visit, for Mr. Clemens' system of eating whenever one felt like it greatly appealed to me, particularly as it never interfered with my regular meals. I seemed to have an insatiable appetite.

We had great fun on our fruit-eating excursions—leaning over the rail, enjoying the delicious fruit. Then, when we had quite finished, we tossed the pits into nature's scrap basket, the chasm below. It was quite exciting to see which one of us could throw the farthest. Mr. Clemens invariably did and it pleased him to win, even though there was no prize. The last act of the plum-eating ritual was wiping our sticky fingers on Mr. Clemens' handkerchief.

Once as we were enjoying our plums, Mr. Clemens said, "I guess we'll have to get someone to take a picture of this." He was expressing what I had often thought. I giggled, because I could see humorous possibilities in such a picture. It was a perfectly spontaneous giggle, but it was at that point a mistake, for it resulted in the picture's never being taken. Mr. Clemens listened to me for a second, then remarked in his slow drawl, "Yes, it certainly would be funny—but I think it might be almost too funny. There's a point where humor verges into the ridiculous and that's something to be avoided. You see, Dorothy, unless you could show both sides, it might look as though we were being seasick!"

So there was never a picture of Mark Twain and me eating plums over the porch rail.

But there were other pictures—plenty of them—for I had brought my camera and even that first morning we took pictures. Mr. Clemens loved to pose, and I snapped him on the porches and in the garden by the nasturtiums. Later, we even made what Mr. Clemens christened, "hunting expeditions," because we did literally hunt for backgrounds.

One day we took pictures of each other near imposing stone pillars that marked the entrance to an estate a little way up the road. First I photographed Mr. Clemens standing in front of the field-stone column, and then he took one of me sitting on top of it. Since it was a rather low, squatty affair with a flat flagstone on its top for a finish, it made a picturesque if not too comfortable seat. Mr. Clemens helped me up and arranged my pose, taking a great deal of care that my long braids should be at just the right angle.

He had just pushed the little bit of steel, which meant the picture was taken, when a car appeared and stopped abruptly. I, of course, seated on the pillar, was quite out of the danger's reach, but Mr. Clemens was standing in the middle of the road in order to get the proper perspective for the picture.

Instead of being nervous or jumpy, as almost anyone would have been at the sudden appearance of the automobile, Mr.

Clemens merely threw back his head and held out his hand in a gesture which was the forerunner of the stop signals the policeman use today. Then quite calmly and deliberately, he stepped over by me, and the way was clear for the car to pass.

But the car did not proceed. Instead, according to apparent instructions, the chauffeur leapt from his seat and held open the door of the tonneau. He helped out a most attractive lady who, by way of coincidence, had a camera in her hand.

She came up to us and proved to be Mrs. Ogden, a friend of Mr. Clemens. I remembered her instantly, for I had met her at the tea. After greetings had been exchanged, she asked if she couldn't take a picture herself as she happened to have a camera.

"Just the thing," exclaimed Mr. Clemens. "You can take a picture of Dorothy and me! Try as we may, we've never been able to do that ourselves. Of course, we keep working at it but we haven't succeeded yet."

So another picture was taken, and I had one more souvenir of my first Tuxedo visit. Long after I returned home, Mr. Clemens sent me an enlargement of the picture Mrs. Ogden took that day. It showed Mr. Clemens and me standing in the roadway, his arm around me, and his beautiful head, which might well have been the model for one of the philosophers of Greece, thrown back as he stood straight and firm. On the picture he wrote:

I think this is the best of the Tuxedo pictures save one, Dorothy dear. Mrs. Ogden made it. I have the bronchitis and am barking at you affectionately.

S. L. C.

I liked it almost as well as any of the other pictures myself, but there was one taken in the garden by Mr. Clemens' secretary that I liked better. It was not Mr. Clemens' favorite. His was one taken on the side porch, where I was standing by his chair. The one that I liked the best was one in which Mr. Clemens said he looked like a "nice old white-headed nigger." The light hadn't been quite right so that Mark Twain's face, being a little shaded, was the ground for his assertion, but it really wasn't so. He looked just like himself, and it was a pose that I so often saw him take, seated with his hand resting on his knee, that I loved it for that reason.

But it was very hard to make a choice of the pictures, for one and all turned out well. Mark Twain was a very photogenic figure, and whenever he posed the results were sure to be satisfactory.

10

Mark Twain at Work

THE DAYS SOON DEVELOPED into a joyous routine. In the mornings, Mr. Clemens worked.

"I'd like to play hooky," he said with one of his gamin expressions, "but on the whole I can't spoil myself too much while you are here. It will make too big a gap when you are gone."

I think the most outstanding moments of my visit were those I spent, quiet as a mouse, listening to Mr. Clemens dictate. He didn't mind having an audience. In fact, he was so absorbed in what he was doing that half the time I do not believe he even knew I was there.

I would tiptoe in and sit in the far corner of the room and listen to him dictating. The watching would be equally as fascinating as the listening; in fact, it could be more so. I never knew the connected threads of the story he was weaving, but the patches were interesting and amusing, as any sentence of his was sure to be, and the manner in which they were delivered was even more delightful.

Nothing interfered with the steady flow of his thoughts. His mind was like a clear crystal spring from which words continually bubbled forth. His dictation was like a mountain stream, swiftly flowing. The sentences came one after the other, with scarcely a pause between.

Mr. Clemens would walk up and down the room while he was dictating, and the dictation sounded more as though he were talking conversationally than creating a story. He would pace back and forth, his hands behind his back, speaking continuously in his slow, drawling way. Often he would say things that the stenographer would think were just funny little by-comments on the story, but which he actually meant to be in the completed manuscript. Thinking they were Mr. Clemens' personal observations or for her own benefit, she would leave them out of the script.

Later, when he had finished dictating and turned to correcting the typed manuscript of the work of the day before, he would discover this and break out into fiery explosions of rage because she had left out something he had particularly wanted in the manuscript. His anger would last several minutes, and then he would calm down very suddenly and dismiss it entirely from his mind, for the time being at any rate.

He had a very difficult time getting it through his stenographers' heads that *every* word he said must go in the story and that they mustn't do any deleting on their own account.

One morning when I had overslept and gotten down too late for the dictation, I found him out on the round porch correcting his manuscript. He was seated on a wicker chair with the pages on his lap and his ever-ready fountain pen in his hand. I have never seen him with a pencil. He always wrote his corrections on the margins of his manuscript in ink. A fountain pen was as much a part of his life as his cigars were, and it seems to me he always had one or the other in his hand.

This morning, when I saw him sitting there working, I crept away and got my camera and tiptoed back and snapped two photographs of him as he corrected his manuscript. I got them just in time, too, for as I took the second picture he put the sheet he had been reading on the chair next to him, on top of the pile of manuscript he had already read, and then turned back to the fresh page. He had barely read more than a few lines when he got up and threw the manuscript down on the chair.

"That girl's done it again!" he exclaimed, and no doubt would have followed the exclamation with much more expressive language, only just at that moment he caught sight of me standing in the doorway and toned it down considerably, as he said later. But he did remark that the stupidity of stenographers was the bane of his life, during a long discourse on the subject in which he worked off a good deal of steam even though he did watch his adjectives for my benefit.

I've often wondered if this difficulty of making his stenographers understand that nothing he said must go unrecorded was why he took to writing himself, instead of dictating, because after Tuxedo I never heard him dictate. In both New York and Redding he wrote his own stories by hand.

After a while, when he had calmed down and given instructions to his secretary that were relayed with a great deal of firmness to the stenographer, I told him I'd taken some pictures of him at work.

"It's a pity you didn't notify me about it, I would have moved my chair into the sunshine. I'm afraid they won't come out, dear."

I, being naturally optimistic, said I was sure they would; one we had taken two days earlier of him on the same upstairs porch, reclining in a chaise longue after a hard morning's work, had turned out very well.

He said he hoped so, but he had a few doubts and was willing to pose again. We moved the chair out into the sunlight and he established himself in it, manuscript in hand, his face toward the camera. I was just ready to click the shutter when I made the discovery that I had used the last film on the roll, and, of course, it was my last roll!

"Never mind, dear heart," Mr. Clemens consoled me. "Tomorrow morning I will take you to the village to buy another roll and get these developed, and if they don't come out, we'll take some more."

My optimism was for once justified. The pictures did come out—a bit hazy, it is true, but a perfect representation of Mark Twain at work.

I I

Manuscripts and Moths Aflutter

EVERY AFTERNOON WE WENT RIDING. But not in an automobile!
No, indeed! We went in state in an open victoria drawn by
a horse, "the noble animal" that Mark Twain immortalized in
"A Horse's Tale."

Automobiles in those days were not the ordinary things
they have since become. They were then at just about the
stage the airplane had reached before World War I. There
weren't very many privately owned ones, and people were still
clinging to the tail end of the horse and buggy era.

Mr. Clemens, himself, was particularly fond of horses and
greatly preferred that means of locomotion to the jouncing
of jiggers, "although in all honesty I must admit they get you
there faster," he said, referring to the taxi-jiggers. "But it's
worth taking longer behind a horse and saving your joints.
Besides, when one wants to see scenery there is nothing so
pleasant as an open carriage."

Every afternoon we rode forth in a low, comfortable vic-

65

toria, and as the horse ambled along over the beautifully wooded roads, Mr. Clemens would lean back in his seat—always on the right hand side—and point out anything he considered at all extraordinary by waving his hand in its direction. The long cigar acted as a pointer, and many a lovely vision I have seen by following its black line.

We would ride along leaving, I am sure, a trail of cigar ashes behind us, for Mr. Clemens smoked incessantly and knocked off the accumulated ash as we went. I often thought of the fairy story of the barley trail left by the man who wanted to find his way home. The birds ate the barley and it proved no help to him. But we were quite secure against this. The birds wouldn't eat the ashes! And if it had been necessary, I am quite sure we could have retraced our way by following Mark Twain's cigar ashes.

Mr. Clemens loved to explore the Park. He was always telling the driver to take us on a new road, and he liked to go down the unfrequented byways. Once on such a jaunt, we passed someone's back yard where the wash was hanging out to dry. They must have been doing a great deal of entertaining, for it seemed to consist mostly of tablecloths and napkins. There were dozens of the latter hanging on the line.

"Look," I exclaimed. "There are your manuscripts hanging out to dry."

Truly they did look like the white sheets of his manuscript paper.

Mr. Clemens drew his eyebrows together.

"Why, Dorothy!" he exclaimed. "Do you think I write the kind of stories that have to be aired?"

I thought I'd said the wrong thing and began to explain the process of my reasoning very seriously. He cut my explanations short.

"No, dear, I don't write that kind. Only once I did, but it's never been aired, or fumigated for that matter. No, my stories don't need airing. They are fresh and pure. You know I've always wanted to be bad but somehow I've never managed it. On the whole, though, I guess it's a good thing because if I had you couldn't have read my books and that would have been a calamity. I often think that the thing that makes me the happiest is that children read and love my books. I am proud that they can.

"One of the things I like about you, Dorothy, is that you, who know them so well, have assured me of that." He paused for a moment to think a little, and as he did so his eye caught the last white glimmer of the wash as we left it behind us. It reminded him of the origin of what he was saying. He leaned over and put his hand on mine. "You're quite right, Dorothy, they do look like manuscripts fluttering in the wind—imagination pinned to the clothes line of life!"

He leaned back in his corner and half closed his eyes, apparently lost in thought. I did not disturb him. I leaned back, too, and watched the scenery.

I know now that the book referred to was *1601*, the Elizabethan conversation that he wrote to shock his friend Dr. Twichell.

There was a spirit of mischief ever lurking in Mark Twain. He liked to astonish people, to amuse them, sometimes even to shock them. I firmly believe that a great many of the sentiments he expressed which have been taken literally as portraying his own viewpoints, were made solely with the tongue-in-cheek motive and didn't express his true feelings at all.

The real Mark Twain was a happy man who loved his work, his friends, and who enjoyed tremendously the pleasures of life; not the embittered, frustrated person so many people have written him down to be. Mark Twain, as I knew him, was neither bitter or frustrated. He was a person who had worked hard for his fame and when he had achieved it delighted in all the things that it brought him.

In the evenings we played games and listened to the orchestrelle. Time for me to go to bed always came too soon, especially after we discovered the fascinating occupation of butterfly-hunting.

It was Mr. Clemens' idea. One evening just as we had finished dinner, I heard a tap-tap on the glass door that went out to the porch.

"Does someone want to come in?" I asked.

Mr. Clemens smiled. "It's a moth that seems to. It sees the light through a crack in the curtain and wants to fly in and beat his wings against it until he dies."

"Oh! That seems silly of it!" I exclaimed.

Mr. Clemens inclined his head. "There's philosophy in it if one takes the time to figure it out."

The tapping was still going on.

"It seems to make too much noise for a moth." I didn't know a great deal about moths, and any that I had seen were far too little to sound like a person knocking.

"They have very big millers and moths here in Tuxedo," Mr. Clemens told me.

"I wish I could see one."

"So you shall. How would you like to collect moths while you're here? We'll put a light in the window off the round porch upstairs to attract them and then we'll catch them and put them to sleep forever with a little chloroform, and mount them in a box." By this time I was as much aflutter as the wings of the moth outside, and I was so eager to get at it that

I would hardly give him time to finish explaining how all this was to be done.

Presently we were all equipped with a small bottle of chloroform, a net which Claude rather miraculously managed to produce, and one of the boxes Mark Twain's manuscript paper came in, which had a layer of cotton neatly laid on the bottom, ready to receive whatever specimen first presented itself. There were also several shiny pins with which to impale the victims, Mr. Clemens carefully explained that the chloroform would be a very easy death, compared to beating their wings off against the light, or being caught in the flame. As a matter of fact, we were really being humane and saving the moths a lot of trouble.

Pretty soon a moth appeared.

Mr. Clemens was afraid to risk the night air for either himself or me, as there was always a certain amount of dampness in the mountains. So he and I stayed inside and watched his secretary do the work of catching the moth and using the chloroform. Then she would bring it inside and mount it in the box.

This grew to be a nightly occupation, along with the music and games. Sometimes when it was very warm and mild, Mr. Clemens and I would join in the hunt.

During one of these butterfly-collecting evenings, I made the discovery that Mark Twain did not like slang. We had just succeeded in capturing a particularly lovely specimen of moth, and after it was properly chloroformed and mounted in the box, I cried out with an excess of admiration, "It's a beaut!" I meant to say "a beauty," but in my excitement over the addition to the collection, I left off the end of the word.

I danced and clapped my hands, repeating, "A beaut—a

beaut!" until I noticed that for once Mr. Clemens was not responding to my enthusiasm. He didn't look cross, but the lines of his face, those deep lines on either side of his mouth, seemed to me to have suddenly deepened.

I broke off my dance, feeling certain that something was wrong. By this time Mr. Clemens had walked over to the window, and his secretary tactfully whispered in my ear that the one thing in the world Mr. Clemens actually detested was slang. "Beaut" was a slang word popular at the time. I hadn't really used it in this sense but merely had been too excited to give the word its second syllable. But I took care never to abbreviate it again or use any other slang expression, as I wouldn't for the world have done anything Mr. Clemens did not like.

One of the letters Mr. Clemens wrote to me after I left Tuxedo mentioned the butterfly-hunting, which had gone on in the daytime as well as at night. The letter began with a picture of a butterfly drawn by Mr. Clemens and went on to say:

SATURDAY

Do you know what this is? It is a butterfly, drawn by the artist, the gifted artist. I am the gifted artist, self-taught.

No. I find it is a grasshopper. It is for your collection. I have nailed it to a box with pins. It took more chloroform than was good for it. And so it is "sleeping with its fathers."

MONDAY A. M.

"Just a week" since I saw you! Why, you little humbug, it is over three months. Even my secretary, who never gets anything straight but cork screws and potato peelings and things like that, concedes that it's upwards of *two* months. What is the matter with your veracity mill?

NIGHT

It is a good idea to choose a name in advance and then fit the literature onto it when it comes. I will keep on lookout for a fortunate name, dear. Write another little story now and send it to me. It will take you several years to learn to do a story even *tolerably* well. Attention and close observation, and ever so much tearing up and re-writing, but no matter, it's worth the trouble and no trade is ever learned well on any other terms.

Good night, it's sleep time.

S. L. C.

12

The Authors' League for Two

REFERENCE TO MY WRITING brings me to the most exciting and far-reaching event of my entire visit at Mark Twain's, the founding of the Authors' League for two, which was the beginning of his teaching me to write.

The Authors' League that Mr. Clemens inaugurated one sunshiny day in Tuxedo was to influence my whole life. It was given birth very dramatically.

As I have said before, Mr. Clemens would often read aloud to me from either his own books or from someone else's.

One day as we were sitting out on the side porch at the garden level, he read me an unfinished story from one of his books. It was a tale he had one of his characters tell for the other people in the story to solve. They couldn't do it any more than the reading public. It was on the order of Frank R. Stockton's "The Lady or the Tiger?" which ended with the hero about to open a door. There were two for him to choose from. Behind one was a beautiful and charming lady, behind the other a ferocious, man-eating tiger. The story ended as he opened the door, and no one ever knew which came out of the portal he had chosen—the lady or the tiger.

Mr. Clemens' story wasn't exactly like that. He merely got his hero into a terribly embarrassing situation. The hero had been held up in the woods as he drove to get his fiancée and robbed of his trousers by a tramp who needed such an article of attire. Seated in the carriage with a lap robe over him, the loss of his nether garments was unnoticed. The young man, after meeting the tramp, drove fast toward his home to get another pair of trousers. Halfway there he met his fiancée, who had gotten tired of waiting for him and had come on with some friends. She decided since they had met and the spot was charming they could picnic right where they were.

The young man, faced with the problem of getting out of the carriage minus his trousers and shocking everyone and probably losing his fiancée, or remaining in the carriage and losing her anyway, watched her growing angrier every second. There were a great many other complications. In fact, Mark Twain had gotten his hero in such a mess that it seemed impossible for him to extricate himself. Whatever he did would plunge him deeper into embarrassment. So the reader was left up in the air for a solution of the hero's difficulties

Mr. Clemens read the story to me and asked me what I thought of it. I pondered over it a little while and finally announced I saw a way the hero could be gotten out of his trouble without losing his girl or being shown up in a bad light before her.

Mr. Clemens said, "Then you write it out, dear."

I retired to a corner of the porch with a pencil and paper and got the hero out of his difficulty by having him, while he was arguing with his fiancée, lean over and stick a pin into the flank of the horse he was driving. Naturally, the horse ran away, providing the hero with an excuse for leaving without his fiancée's breaking the engagement, as she threatened to do if he didn't get out of the carriage.

Once out of sight, he mastered the horse—in my version—got another pair of trousers, put them on, and returned fully clothed to the arms of his beloved. She was so overjoyed to see him after his miraculous escape from the runaway, that she forgot to ask why he had been so stubborn about not getting out of the carriage before.

When I had finished, I took it over and read it aloud, and Mr. Clemens applauded.

I *had* found a way out of the seemingly impossible situation. Mr. Clemens took what I had written, read it aloud himself, and when he had finished laughed immoderately. It was a funny story and I've no doubt my version was even funnier!

Finally Mr. Clemens declared, "There's no doubt about it, you are an author, Dorothy."

I looked up at him as though he were the Delphic oracle. "Oh, do you think I could ever be an author—and really write?" I asked, and waited for his reply more anxiously than any consultant of the famous oracle had ever awaited its pronouncements.

He nodded his head up and down until his white hair looked as though it were being ruffled by a breeze. "Certainly," he said, "anyone with that much imagination would have to be!"

I was overjoyed! Then suddenly I remembered his propensity for teasing and how he was always making jokes. Perhaps this was one of them. I could tell if I could see his eyes. If there were a twinkle in them I would know he was fooling, but he was nodding his head and I couldn't look into his eyes to read the truth.

"Do you really mean it? You're not fooling me? Do you really think I could write stories and books?" I insisted.

He stopped nodding and looked at me very seriously. "Yes, Dorothy, I do," he replied, and I knew that he was not joking and that he really meant what he was saying. There was no impish twinkle in his eyes; instead a fire of enthusiasm was shining forth, and this his words carried on.

"I do think so, and I am glad. Now we will start an Authors' League—two authors together. We will work hard, and I shall teach you what I know—and you will teach me too."

My heart was beating in double-quick time at the idea of Mark Twain's teaching me to write and actually thinking it was worth while to do so.

The Authors' League—it sounded too wonderful to be an actuality! I didn't mind hard work. I would love it with Mr. Clemens for a taskmaster.

All at once through my excitement the significance of his last words struck me, "and you will teach me too." I regarded him wonderingly. I didn't understand. Why, Mark Twain knew everthing. He was looked up to by the whole world!

"But I can't teach *you* anything," I said.

"Oh, yes you can," Mark Twain replied. "You can teach me how to be young, dear."

So a little girl took her first wavering uncertain flights into the realm of writing, with the celebrated Mark Twain for her guide.

Soon the literary atmosphere had entirely encompassed me so that I even wanted to try to see if I could dictate. Mr. Clemens obligingly offered his services as amanuensis.

"I know just how it should be done by long experience," he said, and added. "You might as well profit by my knowledge and you don't need to worry that I'll leave anything out!"

He was referring once again to the stenographer whose "stupidity," as he termed it, still rankled.

During the rest of my stay the Authors' League was in session at least two hours every day. I would generally write a little story in the morning while Mr. Clemens was working. Then when he had finished and came downstairs, he would either read what I had written or have me read it to him. Then he would point out the faults and have me do the story over and over until it was "as good as it can be," which expression of his placed the final seal of his approval on my effort.

He promised to look out for a nom de plume for me. He had chosen his own with great care—a souvenir of his pilot days on the Mississippi River, when he had so often heard the men on the river steamboats calling out, "Mark Twain, mark twain," as they measured the depth of the river by knotted ropes.

His pilot days were among the happiest of his life, and it was poignant that part of the times he loved so much was symbolizing his achievement. "Mark Twain"—in that name the river he knew so well was still with him. He had chosen it because he thought it would be a good name to use for his writing, and it had certainly justified his thinking.

He told me he would find a name equally as good for me, but later on he decided that my own would be the most effective name I could use because "it has an arresting quality."

One of the first stories I ever wrote was a goody-goody little tale entitled, "What the Oak Tree Saw," about a little boy who wanted to play hooky from school. I dictated it to Mr. Clemens, and he was very pleased with it. After I went home he wrote and asked me to send it back to him.

While the Authors' League flourished, it didn't monopolize all the time any more than Mr. Clemens' own work did; for in addition to the hours given over to amusement and the afternoon drives, Mr. Clemens took me to a great many parties. Everyone in Tuxedo wanted to entertain the celebrity in their midst, and a great many of the residents of the Park were friends of Mark Twain's who delighted to do him honor. So hardly a day went by without our attending a function of some sort.

It was fun going places with Mark Twain and being made much of. I wouldn't have been human if I hadn't enjoyed it. But best of all I loved being with him when the Authors' League was in progress, or when he was reading aloud. The latter was especially interesting to me, for when he read his own books he would often stop and explain just what had made him write that particular story. Or if the episode was one portraying an incident of his own youth, he would tell me so and go into great detail about it, which happened very often when the book he was reading was *Tom Sawyer*.

Sometimes, when his voice grew tired, his secretary would continue the reading or I would take a turn at it myself, which delighted him. He mentioned my reading aloud in one of his letters written shortly after I had left.

TUXEDO PARK, NEW YORK
SUNDAY, AUG. 11

This isn't a letter, Dorothy dear. Yet I know I ought to write you a letter because I said I would write you every time I wrote the other children, and I've just finished a letter to Clara. But I never could keep promises very well. However, I shall certainly write you a letter before very long.

I wrote to Clara: "When Dorothy went away she took the sun and the moon and the constellations with her left silence and solitude and night and desolation behind her."

And *that's* a true word, if ever *I've* spoken true word!

77

THURSDAY, 15TH

I have been away several days but am home again—and no Dorothy! And so I go mourning around, like an old cat that's lost her kitten. But you are coming soon again and that is a large comfort to me. You are the best reader of your age I have yet encountered, and when I finish teaching you, you will read still better than you do now. It's a great accomplishment, a very great and very rare accomplishment and *I'm* the expert that knows how to teach it. There'll be grand times in my class of one pupil, Dorothy dear.

Thank you for your letter which was very sweet and welcome. I am glad you arrived safe—you and the other butterflies, and the turtle with the warlike name.

A wonderful thing has happened here. You remember the central bed of nasturtiums, the round one? Well, we planted some seeds there and raised a family of rabbits. The nest is under the nasturtiums in the middle of the bed. There are three little rabbits and they are about the size of mice. Their eyes are not open yet. I hope they will still be there when you come. I have named them Dorothy. One name is enough for all of them. They are so little. Your friend,

SLC

So writing wasn't the only thing that Mark Twain taught me. From him I learned reading and writing; but I learned even more than that, for I learned, too, the simplicity that goes with true greatness and it was a lesson that I never forgot.

13

Gifts of Books and an Elephant

THE VERY DAY after I had returned home I received a letter from Mark Twain signed by the name I had chosen, SLC.

TUXEDO PARK
FRIDAY EVENING

Dorothy dear,

One of these days I am going to write you a letter the first time I write my other children, but not now, for I haven't anything to do and I can't write letters except when I am rushed.

I went to bed as soon as you departed, there being nothing to live for after that, and the sunshine all gone. How do you suppose I am going to get along without you? For five hours this has been a dreary place, a sober and solemn place, a hushed and brooding and lifeless place, for the blessed spirit of youth has gone out of it and left nothing that's worthwhile. Aren't you sorry for me, you fresh breeze blown from fragrant fields of flowers? I thought this was a home. It was a superstition. What is home without a child? Particularly a house that's had such a child as you in it.

It isn't a home at all, it's merely a wreck. *Now* I hope you see what you've done by going away, you little witch.

It's odd, this morning I dated that "recommend" August 5 instead of 9. I think it is because you seemed to have been here only one day—just one short beautiful day—without a break in it. I am very grateful to your Mother for loaning you to me, you dear sweet child, I am aware that you can't come again in August but I hope you can come after Sept. 2nd and stay a *whole* week, not a broken one. I mean to expect it and count upon it and I do hope I shall not have to make any engagements that would interfere.

Are you an idol? I suspect it, for I know you have left a lot of idolators behind you in this house, of whom the very principalist one is the undersigned.

Please give my kindest regards to all your household.

SLC

It is always delightful to be missed, so naturally this letter made me very happy and I promptly wrote back and told Mr. Clemens how much I missed him. At the same time my letter came, Mother received one from him in which he said, "Every day and hour of her brief stay Dorothy was a delight and a blessing and every night it cost me a pang to let her go to bed." He finished with how pleased he had been that I hadn't been homesick. He wrote, "Homesickness is a dreadful malady. I can still remember the nostalgia of it after all these years."

In this letter he also made the arrangements for my next visit, which was planned for September 3. Since I didn't want to be away from Mother on my birthday, which was the first day of the month, we chose the nearest date to it. This time I had no worry about being homesick, only a joyous anticipation of returning to my elderly friend.

In a letter dated Wednesday, August 21, Mr. Clemens mentioned both the proposed visit and my birthday. The letter

began with a fascinating picture of a bee chasing something—
just what, even the "gifted artist" himself wasn't quite sure:

About tomorrow or the next day there'll be a note from the
same, I hope, containing the picture of the same and me which
the same kodaked when the same was here. I suppose you will
return to Plainfield for your birthday.

That thing the bee is chasing is a dog or a rat or something of
that kind, I think, but there is room for conjecture. This does not
settle it. What do you think it is, if you've got time.

You are coming Tuesday, the 3rd. Now, then, *that's* settled,
Lassie. Shall you be welcome? There isn't any doubt about it, dear.

AFTERNOON

The Harpers have sent the books here. It's just as well. I will
write my name in them, then forward them.

THURSDAY, AUGUST 22ND

I'm collecting old cigar belts for you against your coming—but
I love you notwithstanding.

SLC.

There had been one roll of films that had been taken the
day before I left which I had brought home to be developed.
But I had delayed sending them to him, which was very
naughty, especially when he'd been so thoughtful about saving
the cigar bands for me. He knew that I was trying to get
enough red ones together to make a tray.

The books of which he spoke arrived shortly after his letter
and although it wasn't my birthday, I couldn't resist opening
the big package. To my delighted eyes, once I had ripped off
the outer wrappings, there were revealed ten of Mark Twain's
own books, all autographed. He had picked out the ones he
thought most suitable for me—those I already knew and loved.
There were *Tom Sawyer, Huckleberry Finn, A Connecticut
Yankee in King Arthur's Court, Innocents Abroad, A Tramp*

Abroad, The Prince and The Pauper, Eve's Diary, and *Joan of Arc.* The latter, of all the books he had written, was not only his favorite but "the one *I* want to be remembered by," he had told me on the steamer. He also sent me two collections of his short stories.

They were all bound in bright red, my favorite color. I had never had such a wonderful birthday present or one I valued more highly. I almost wore them out looking at them before the day which they were intended to celebrate arrived.

I wrote Mr. Clemens how much I loved his gift and at the same time asked if I might read "A Dog's Tale." In reply came another of his illustrated letters:

TUXEDO PARK
NEW YORK
MONDAY, AUG. 26/07

At last, you dear ittle tardy rascal! This morning I was going to stick up a notice on the back porch:

LOST CHILD!
Answers to the name of Dorothy.
Strayed, stolen or mislaid.
DISAPPEARED
on or about the 9th of August.
anyone returning this inestimably precious
asset to the
S O R R O W I N G
will be richly
R E W A R D E D !

and right away this evening came your letter and takes every bit of the uneasiness away from me! I had gone to bed but my secretary brought it anyway because she knew I would break her furniture and throw all her things out of the window if she delayed it till morning. Very well, you have been having good times; so I am satisfied and will go to sleep now.

But wait! Where is that picture of you and me? You have forgotten it, dear, but I must have it.

TUESDAY

Yes. Wednesday will be perfectly convenient and we'll have you for a whole week, which is grand! Provided you don't get homesick—and we do hope you won't. We'll do our best to keep you happy and content. My secretary will arrange about the trains with your Mother by telegraph if she can, otherwise by letter. I've got a birthday ——— for you ——— but I will keep it till you come, because it isn't the ——— and I shall need to ——— (*guess what it is*). You've written me a good letter, simple, lucid, straightforward, well-expressed.

(Picture)
Flight of the rabbit family.

Alas! They have deserted us and I am so sorry. We were hoping to keep them for you and we never dreamed that they would go away and leave us. I am just as sorry as I can be. That big one that has three ears and looks like an angel, isn't an angel at all. It is the Mother rabbit. She isn't swimming. She is praying, praying for succor, I reckon. That is I *think* that that is her idea. No, that isn't it! She is jumping—jumping over a rope, walk, or a stone wall, or something of that kind, and has bumped her stomach against it, poor thing. It is very difficult to tell what a rabbit is really trying to do in a picture, because rabbits are so irrelevant. It is their nature when excited.

Do I mind? (That you read "The Dog's Tale.") Indeed no. I don't mind anything you do, because you never mean any harm, and you are a dear, good child all the time.

You have written the *very letter* I was going to propose that you write; a letter telling me about your activities and industries and enjoyments—all the things your busy hands and head find to interest themselves in. It is good practice for you, in observing and remembering and good entertainment for me because I am fond of you and so whatever you do and think and feel interests me.

83

You are coming Tuesday; It's fine. You will reach this house at
5:30 P. M. You will most certainly be welcome.

(Picture)

Deer.

There were several of them. They came down hill from the
woods above the house and stopped awhile behind the kitchen
to look at the cook. You can see by their eager expression and
enthusiastic delight that they had never seen a cook before. Sometimes they go down through the woods below the house to get a
drink at the lake. If they ever come into the house you must be
ready, for we will have them to luncheon and then photograph
them in the act.

With love and good night.

SLC

I was terribly sorry to hear of the flight of the rabbit family,
for I had been looking forward to seeing my namesakes. But
I was so intrigued over the prospect of having deer to luncheon
that it quite took the edge off my disappointment over the
rabbits.

"A Dog's Tale" had been a great temptation to me—as great
as Pandora's box had been to her. Unlike Pandora, I did not
peep; I waited until I had permission to do so. But once it
was received, I lost no time in reading the book, and as Mr.
Clemens had predicted, my heart was wrung by its pathos. I
cried long and bitterly over the little dog, and when later I
confessed my tears to Mr. Clemens, he said, "I knew you'd be
affected, but at least I wasn't there to see you and a good cry
once in a while doesn't hurt anyone—especially if it's in a
good cause."

One of the stories of Mark Twain's that I had most enjoyed

84

hearing him read aloud when I was in Tuxedo was that delicious satire on detectives, *The Stolen White Elephant,* over which we had laughed and laughed. Most of the satire I was too young to understand, but I loved the description of the elephant. I had said that elephants always fascinated me and told him of my first experience at a circus when I was only four.

I had been terribly frightened by the clowns with their pistols and funny antics, and at the first opportunity I slipped out of our box. Later my Mother, to her great amazement, found the child that had screamed in terror over the harmless clowns, sitting contentedly patting one of the elephants, with an amused keeper watching to see I came to no harm.

"That was very brave of you, Dorothy," Mr. Clemens had remarked, "and I wouldn't have thought it of you either, the way you ran away from that caterpillar!"

"Oh, that's different. I can't stand caterpillars, and I *like* elephants." I told him very seriously. "I'd like to have an elephant for a pet if they only weren't so big."

And then the conversation had been changed and I'd forgotten all about it. But Mark Twain hadn't, for on the morning of my birthday I received a wire from him.

Miss Dorothy Quick
                                                    PLAINFIELD, NEW JERSEY
I tried to get some elephants for your birthday but they charged ten thousand dollars a piece. I can get one elephant or sixteen hundred monkeys for the same money if you prefer. Telephone answer.

                                                    SLC

When I couldn't get through on the wire to him, I sent a telegram in reply and said I'd rather have the books he'd sent me than all the elephants and monkeys in the world. But when

85

I returned to Tuxedo, almost the first thing he gave me was the present he had been so mysterious about in his letter. It turned out to be a small white ivory elephant, so I had an elephant for my very own after all!

14

Advice on Poetry for an Indian Princess

WHEN I WENT to Tuxedo for my second visit, I traveled on the train. I could hardly wait for it to ease itself into the station, I was so anxious to see SLC again.

He was there waiting on the platform, his eyes shining as he waved a welcome.

It wasn't long before I was off the train, running toward him, and the journey from the jigger to the friendly mansion on the side of the cliff was like a happy progress.

It seemed almost as though there had been no intervening time between my visits; I slipped into my place in the household just as though I had never been away at all, except that I had lots to talk about and lots to hear, for the charms of the rabbit family were put on parade for my benefit until I declared it didn't seem fair that they had left before I came. Mr. Clemens said he'd see if he couldn't plant some more seeds and raise another crop for my benefit. "Although it's not often that one can repeat anything so unique," he mused sadly.

This visit was very much a repetition of the first except that it was longer and was packed even fuller with joyousness. We took more photographs, and the Authors' League flourished to even a greater degree than it had before. There wasn't a day that passed that I didn't either write a story or dictate one to Mr. Clemens, and he would, with mock sternness, see that I worked over them until they were "as near right as they can be until you've gotten to be at least half my age, Dorothy."

I wrote one story about an Indian princess, and Mr. Clemens read it aloud to his secretary. Then he made a few suggestions, and after I had carried them out according to his satisfaction, he read it again, pointing out my progress with much pride. He would never make any changes himself in anything I did, but he would point out what was wrong and then leave me to make it right, which he said was excellent practice.

After the final reading of the Indian princess story, he asked how I would like to illustrate it. I thought that would be simply grand, so he said he would take a picture of me in an Eastern costume to go with the story. There was a great deal of running to and fro to procure costume materials, for Mr. Clemens wanted it to be just right, and, like his character in "Adam's Diary," he did love to superintend.

"It's so easy to tell people what to do and watch them doing it, and then if it goes wrong you can always put the blame on them, dear heart," he often told me.

Eventually the things were all assembled and I retired with Mr. Clemens' secretary to make ready for a grand entrance. I had a tan linen dress with heavy red embroidery about the neck and short sleeves. This was used as a foundation. Then a long length of mirror-embroidered material was wrapped around me for a skirt in true Balinese fashion, fastened at the waist with a jeweled girdle. My long braids were wound around

88

my head in a very grown-up manner and fastened so that the
red hair ribbons I wore on their ends made bows over each
ear that looked like flaming red poppies. Then a headband that
matched the jeweled girdle was put across my forehead, and
rows and rows of bright colored beads were hung around my
neck. Long turquoise chiffon veils were draped over all this
and allowed to trail yards after me on the ground, until I
looked like a veritable rani of old India.

But the most exciting part, as far as I was concerned, was
yet to come. Mr. Clemens' secretary made up my face to complete the picture, and when I saw my elongated eyes, beaded
lashes, rouged cheeks, and crimson mouth, I felt as though a
complete metamorphosis had taken place; I was no longer a
little girl play-acting, but the actual princess I was supposed
to represent.

I paraded for Mr. Clemens as proudly as a peacock and then,
with the concrete wall of the side of the house for a background, I posed for my picture. When it had been taken from
several angles and the camera put away, I said that I wished
I could dress like that all the time.

Mr. Clemens surveyed me and shook his head. "That would
never, never do. Imagine going for a walk in that tight skirt
with all those fripperies! But I wish that there was such a
thing as color photography so that those rich reds and that
heavenly shade of turquoise blue need not be lost. Some day
they will have color photography," he prophesied, "but that
won't help us now. Still, I will advance the times myself. I
have a friend who is an artist and I will get him to color the
picture with water color paints, which will be almost as good.
Anyway, we may as well think so."

The picture turned out to be a great success when it was
developed. Mr. Clemens christened it "The Indian Princess,"

89

and had it enlarged, tinted, and hung in his billiard room. He always cherished it.

In one of his letters after I had gone home, he mentioned the story:

Tuxedo Park, New York
Thursday, Sept. 12/07

Dorothy dear, you are gone and I am dissatisfied.

Friday

You are still gone and I am still dissatisfied.

Subsequently

You are still gone and I am still more dissatisfieder than ever. This is a long day.

> *Homeward the bandit plods her weary way*
> *And leaves the world to darkness and to me.*

I will go to bed.

Saturday

Which I did. But a cricket was hiding somewhere in the room and continuously and monotonously shrieking. I endured it an hour (until ten) then removed to another room. I returned at 11, at 1, and at 4, but was driven out each time.

Last night he drove me out at 9:30 and I returned no more.

— — — — —

Meantime, your letter has come, you very dear child, and I think it is the best typewritten handwriting I have ever seen. I would not have believed a type machine could spell so well. I'm a-missing you, Dorothy.

(Picture of cricket.)
(And three pictures of an axe.)
(Anyway I think it's an axe but some think it's a bonnet.)

But it's for that cricket when I get him. I am quite certain as to that.

I'm going to Fairhaven, Mass., day after tomorrow—Monday—and return Thursday night.

Advice on Poetry for an Indian Princess

I sail for Jamestown three days later to be gone several days.

— — — — —

I've had a misfortune, dear. A page of the Indian story is missing. I shall find it, but meantime I want you to re-write it—it's good practice—and send it here. With lots of love, you dear little rascal.

SLC

The "typewritten handwriting" of which he speaks was printing. He had complained that my scrawl was difficult to read, so I had printed the whole letter for the joke of it. But as usual it was impossible to get ahead of Mr. Clemens.

The quotation from the "Elegy in the Country Churchyard" was very apt. I had learned it during my visit to surprise my grandfather when I got home. This poem was one of which he was particularly fond and from which he was always quoting excerpts. Mr. Clemens would hear me recite the verses I had learned, and when finally I had mastered the whole and would repeat it from beginning to end, he said I had certainly achieved something. The poem was very long for a little girl, and he hoped I would learn something to recite to him when I came "a-visiting at No. 21 Fifth Avenue." I eagerly promised, only I stipulated that I would not pick out such a long one to learn ever again, and Mr. Clemens said that was all right so far as he was concerned. He thought he would enjoy a short one just as much, if not more, because "I've always thought, Dorothy, that there is something about a long poem that acts as a narcotic, no matter how good it is. So if you ever take to verse making, be sure your poems are short and have something in them that will make people take notice. That will keep them awake, and then they'll be sure to remember you, dear."

15

A June Bug and the Bird of Paradise

DURING THIS VISIT Mark Twain read aloud, *A Connecticut Yankee in King Arthur's Court*. Hearing that book in his own mellow tones was an experience that I shall never forget.

He often stopped reading to explain bits about the narrative. He told me that the whole idea had come to him in a dream in which he, himself, was back in King Arthur's Court yet kept a complete remembrance of his nineteenth-century character; the dream had amused him so much that he had carried it ever farther into a book. "That finished all the floweriness of chivalry, Dorothy, and showed the knights as they really were, stripped of all that romantic nonsense. It took me several years and a great deal of study to achieve it."

"Study?" I was astonished that Mark Twain, who knew so much, should have to study. This was beyond my comprehension.

"Of course. I studied the old legends, the history, the customs. Writing isn't all play, dear heart. Sometimes even I have to work over it," he drawled, and then went on even slower, with the laugh lines about his eyes deepening. "You see, you can't expect to achieve anything without work, and the more you put into it the better it will be. Only be sure, dear, to hold just a little back always, so the public will want more! That's one thing no writer can afford to forget—their public. If they do, pretty soon they find they haven't got any."

One day while he was reading, a Mrs. North came to call. When she heard what had been going on, she begged Mr. Clemens not to stop, for she wanted to hear, too. So her call was spent in listening to two chapters, and when finally she left, she said that nothing so delightful had ever happened to her before and she wished she could change places with me and hear the whole book.

That was one wish I was very glad couldn't be fulfilled. I didn't want to relinquish my place to anyone.

One of the things Mr. Clemens most looked forward to during the day was the arrival of the mail. It was a constant source of enjoyment to him. He said, "Letters are like a plum pudding—you never know when you might come across a plum, and though sometimes you might crack your tooth on a bit of a nut shell that got in by mistake, the succulent plums quite made up for any temporary inconvenience."

He often read me letters that came to him with requests for autographs, books and assistance. One man wrote he had known him out West and that since "Sam" now had so much money, he was sure "Sam" wouldn't miss some, so would he please send him enough to live on. Mr. Clemens had never heard of the man and instructed his secretary not to bother to answer. But to another man who wrote that he was one of the friends of a friend of Sam Clemens in those Western days, he sent an autographed copy of *Roughing It*, because he remem-

93

bered once having heard his friend mention that particular man.

The obviously insincere letters were unanswered but all others were carefully taken care of. Mr. Clemens read each one himself and was always very generous about sending his autograph, and he was very pleased at the number of requests he received for his signature.

Inspired by hearing numerous requests for autographs each day, I thought it would be a good idea for me to start a collection myself. Looking back, I seem to have been quite a collector in my youth! The interest in butterflies had been exhausted during my first visit. Since my return we hadn't once had the butterfly net out. Mark Twain said, "So you're going to substitute the pen for a net. Well, after all, the idea is much the same. I'll tell you how to draw them in, dear heart; because if there's anything that makes me mad and likely to refuse a request it's a long rambling letter that wears you out before you get to the point. Now, I'll tell you what to write and make out an example, and if you use it I'll wager you'll never be refused. Only be sure you send a stamped self-addressed envelope along. People always feel a sense of responsibility if they see a stamp and there are very few mean enough to take it off and use it themselves. And if they are, then you don't want their autograph."

He sat right down, pulled his fountain pen out of the upper vest pocket where he always kept it, and in a few seconds he had produced a letter for me to go by:

Dear ——

Will you please send your autograph to a little girl who is anxious to add it to her collection?

DOROTHY QUICK

I immediately adopted it and Mr. Clemens prediction was justified, for I never had a refusal.

Mr. Clemens said that I should have a personal autograph book for my friends to write in, so he, himself, took me down to the village to purchase a small black leather-bound book of blank pages.

As soon as we had gotten back to the house, he wrote on the very first page:

To Dorothy,
Consider well the proportions of things. It is better to be a young June bug than an old Bird of Paradise.

MARK TWAIN

and in the corner:

To Dorothy, with the love of SLC. SEPT. /07.

The next day Colonel Harvey arrived for lunch, and afterward Mr. Clemens whispered, "You'd better get the Colonel to write in your book."

I ran upstairs and came down, album in hand, and proffered my request. The Colonel read what his distinguished friend had written, and then wrote:

If it be so—which I question—then why the necessity of considering well?

GEORGE HARVEY

To Dorothy with the recollection of one of my own.

This lese majesty occasioned a great deal of argument between the two men, which for the most part was over my head. It went on and on, but in the end Mark Twain carried off his point with flying colors, although the Colonel didn't change what he had written.

Eventually the whole book was filled with comments on what Mark Twain had said on the first page.

One day I noticed a great deal of preparation going on; it was far more than I had seen for any visitor—even the Colonel. So I thought someone of great fame, or perhaps an important editor, was coming to visit.

When I asked Mr. Clemens, he said he expected a "Representative of the Press." I looked surprised and he immediately asked why.

"I thought surely it was someone of great importance," I replied honestly.

"You were quite right. It is. Always remember that in America there is nothing so important to a person in the public's eye as the Press."

The orchestrelle wasn't by any means neglected in the midst of our games and good times. There was hardly a day or an evening that it wasn't played. I even got so I could do it myself, and Mr. Clemens often asked me to play it for him.

"I like the way you modulate it, you little rat. You have a sense of rhythm that will help you to write, even though you may not think the two things go together."

One day when I was playing a roll on the orchestrelle and pretending I was actually bringing the music from the keys by moving my hands over them, a lady happened to call on Mr. Clemens. She said, "It doesn't seem possible a child could play the organ like that." As the piece I was playing had been recorded by Josef Hofmann, I don't wonder at her doubt!

Mr. Clemens made no explanation. He only smiled and remarked, "Dorothy does everything beautifully," and the lady didn't know him well enough to discern the telltale twinkle in his eyes. He took good care, however, to maneuver her out on the porch so that she couldn't see me remove the roll at the end or hear the click it made. Later, when the caller had gone, we had a good laugh over the joke.

All at once a thought struck me, and I pointed out that it wouldn't be quite so funny if sometime someone asked me to play on an organ that didn't have any records. Then certainly I wouldn't be able to live up to the reputation given me. Mr. Clemens pulled at his drooping moustache until it stood out straight with a very dashing air, and said. "Then you must seize the moment to develop temperament and refuse to play on any instrument but mine."

And we both agreed that we had solved the problem.

We took more pictures, and Mark Twain posed for me in his Oxford gown. There were more teas, more luncheons, and altogether I had such a good time that it wasn't necessary to coax me very hard to stay longer. So I had ten days with Mark Twain instead of a week, and during the entire time he never went anywhere that he couldn't take me with him, except one dinner that was being given in his honor and had been planned long before I had even met him.

When I saw him dressed in his white evening clothes with a white cape hung picturesquely around his shoulders, I was glad he had had to go as otherwise I would have missed seeing him looking like a cavalier of other days; and when the next day he put on the cape so I could add this picture to the others I had, I was more pleased than ever.

But at last the ten perfect days were over. Mr. Clemens wanted me to stay even longer and I certainly wanted to, but I was going to school for the first time in my life that fall. I was looking forward to it with mixed emotions. I had always had a governess at home, but now Mother had decided that it would be better for me to go to school. I was entered at the Plainfield Seminary, which opened on September 15, so my visit couldn't be prolonged any further.

But I had the prospect of staying with Mr. Clemens at his New York home when he returned to town in the very near future, which I felt would make up to a large extent for the terrors of school.

Mr. Clemens said he couldn't go to the station with me this time, because now that he knew I wouldn't be coming back it would make him feel too badly. So I kissed him good-by and went off in the jigger, waving my hand frantically to the white-clad figure standing on the porch where we had had such good times together. As we drove away, for a long time I could see the sunlight making a nimbus of his white hair.

16

Captain Stormfield, *Geometry,*
and St. Nicholas

WHILE I STAYED WITH HIM, Mark Twain had been dictating *Captain Stormfield's Visit to Heaven,* and having heard scattered bits of it as he gave them birth, I was very anxious to read the entire story.

Fortunately for me, his secretary, who was taking me to my mother in New York, had to deliver the manuscript of *Captain Stormfield* to Mr. Clemens' publishers, Harper and Brothers, on the same trip. On the way down she counted the words in the story once more, to be sure no mistake had been made in the total. This was very important as Mark Twain was paid by the word, and thirty cents a word amounted to a lot on such a long story as *"Captain Stormfield's Visit to Heaven.*

Mr. Clemens was paid for each word in his original manuscript, so that even if some of it were blue-penciled by an editor, it made no difference to the author financially. In fact, Mark Twain once said that he put in things for editors to take out because he knew they weren't happy unless they could use their blue pencil.

After the words on a page were counted, it was handed over to me and I read it avidly. Of course, a great many of the nuances were entirely beyond my comprehension, but I was very proud of the fact that I was the first person, excepting Mark Twain and his secretary, who had read it. And I felt even cockier when it created such a to-do in the literary world on its publication.

The trip down under such circumstances seemed over almost before it had begun. I had just time to finish the story before the train pulled into the station. But when once I saw Mother, I forgot everything else. On the trip out to Plainfield my tongue went faster than the train's wheels, I was so busy recounting the good times I had had in Tuxedo.

I received the letter that I called the "dissatisfied letter" shortly after my return and was glad to know I was missed by my friend. His next letter reported on his trip and the cricket which had been keeping him awake nights.

TUXEDO PARK, NEW YORK
SEPT. 26/07

Dorothy dear,

I hear that you are at school and that you greatly like it and are very busy—all of which is good to hear and naturally is a great pleasure and comfort to your Mother. I am back from Jamestown and am glad. Still we had reasonable weather and a swift voyage and altogether a good time, and enjoyed the trip. Meantime the cricket has joined the union and cleared out. This room is quiet now.

Delia's gone. She meant well but she wasn't of much account and was a trouble breeder with the other servants. Maggie is back and now it's a model household. In about a week Catherine will be back from Ireland. *She's* a bird!

It is milking time now. I mean, I am taking my noon-day glass of milk. Several drops have gone down the wrong way. Try it. It is ever so much fun.

I miss you, dear—I miss you a *lot*. If I had you here we would start the Authors' League again.

Some ladies are calling and I must go down and see them. Good-bye.

SLC

(And then he drew an inimitable picture of one of the ladies.)

As he said, I had started school and had found it to be not nearly as bad as I expected. In fact, it was rather fun and I was enjoying it, except for mathematics. I never had a head for figures, and arithmetic proved to be the bête noire. The very thought of geometry was so terrifying to me that when I made a report on my schoolwork to Mr. Clemens that winter, I declared I would give up the idea of graduating rather than struggle with geometry, as I couldn't see any sense in knowing it anyway. No one ever used it in everyday life.

Mr. Clemens shook his head and pronounced wisely. "Oh, no, you mustn't do that, Dorothy. Why, the only thing that's the matter with me is that I never studied geometry. If I had I would have been President by now. You must go on with your arithmetic and algebra and geometry and graduate with flying colors."

For once I didn't see eye to eye with him, and he must have read my mind. My face, I am quite sure, reflected my uncertainty, for before I could voice it, he added, "Besides, anyone who wants to be an author must study geometry. It may not seem to be of any use, and I must admit it isn't of much account when it comes to adding up bills, but nevertheless, the study of it makes the mind quick and alert and that is good training for a writer."

By now he had actually worked up some enthusiasm for the bogey in my mind, which was what he had set out to do. When, after thinking a few minutes, I announced that I would do my best to struggle with the nasty little figures and graduate for his sake, he was very pleased and said, "I shall come and see you do it, Dorothy dear, and be the first to congratulate you."

When my graduation day came he was no longer here to keep his promise, but I was glad I had achieved the thing he wanted and was grateful to him for working so hard to have me do it that day in New York when the subject of geometry first came up.

In October I received a letter in answer to one of mine complaining that I hadn't heard from him for a whole long week and telling me about a photograph I had sent him of myself on my way to school.

OCT. 2

It is a very good photograph, Dorothy dear, and I am very glad to have it. Wish I could have you here too. I miss you all the time. Goodness! What makes you think I have forgotten you? Indeed I haven't, but I have been so busy lately that I haven't written to my daughters and they are scolding me. I hope to do better now and be good, for a while. It will attract attention. I like that.

I'll be back in New York just at the end of this month and then I hope you can come to us on Saturdays and stay over. We can have very good times together.

OCT. 3

Last night we played "Hearts"—a very good game, I think, because it is simple and doesn't require any mental labor. I wish we had thought of it when you were here. But next time we'll play it. It is more interesting than those other games.

You should see our cat. It is half grown and is gay and wise and courteous and very handsome. It has a tail at one end and two sets of legs, one set at the bow and the other at the stern, and is just as astonishing in other ways.

Then he drew a picture of the cat at a very "fetching" angle. In fact, it looked like it was about to go for a ride down a chute and was enjoying the prospect very much. Under the picture he went on to say:

This cat is trying to look like my secretary but I think it does not succeed very well—and won't until it has had more practice. It sits up like this. Always on the same end. Everybody admires it and thinks it is full of talent.

We drove over the Wigger Pond Road and all around the lake yesterday afternoon. Remember that road? It is very beautiful now. We'll make a longer drive today. I wish you were here to go with us.

EVENING

Your letter and the pictures have come, dear. The one where you are standing by my chair is the very, *very* best one of you I have ever seen and you are next best in the one where I am a nice old white-headed nigger. That little cat caught a bird today and brought it in and it got away and flew out of the window.

There is a heavenly dog here, but he is not ours. He came down the hill on a visit and will have to be sent back. He is the long kind. With love.

SLC.

And then there was a picture of the dog, which ran the whole length of the page to emphasize the fact that he decidedly was the "long kind."

Although I was busy at school and with my homework, I hadn't forgotten the Authors' League. I still went on writing stories, keeping them to take in to Mr. Clemens when he came back to New York.

One of these stories which I had worked over particularly hard, I was quite pleased with, and I thought how wonderful it would be if I could get it published. If a magazine would take it and print it, how delighted SLC would be! How proud of his pupil!

My knowledge of magazines was limited, but the one magazine with which I was thoroughly familiar was *St. Nicholas,* and they were running a contest for short stories by children under twelve. I wrote out the tale in my best "typewritten handwriting" and sent it in and waited with my heart in my mouth for the result. I could hardly study my lessons, I was so busy watching for the postman.

At last the magazine arrived. I turned quickly to the contest announcements. I hadn't won a prize, so my story wasn't published, but I had won an honorable mention for my story and there was my name, "Dorothy Quick," in print, for the first time in connection with an effort of my own.

I was so thrilled, so proud and excited, and half of it was over the anticipation of how pleased Mr. Clemens would be over the success of his pupil. I got another copy of the *St. Nicholas* and marked a red circle around my name and sent it to him. I could hardly contain my excitement as I waited for his reply.

Finally it came—the last letter I was to receive from him— postmarked Tuxedo.

TUXEDO PARK, NEW YORK

Dorothy dear,
It is perfectly lovely here now, with brilliant skies, brilliant water, sleek as a mirror, and all the brilliant colors of the hills

painted on it like a picture, and there's rabbits, oh, no end! They've got a nest in that tree that leans over the nasturtium bed and they scamper up and down it all day long and jabber. And as for squirrels and deer and Italians and other game, they're everywhere and nobody shoots them for it isn't allowed. I don't know why. And there are owls and cows and bears and nights you can hear them hooting. Sometimes they make the kind of noise a preacher makes. It is awful, but I am not afraid. The others are afraid, but I am calm and go down cellar.

I believe that that is about all the news there is, except that we leave Tuxedo the 31st to live in town, 21 Fifth Avenue, where you must come and stay over Sundays every time you can be spared.

Dear heart, you mustn't send stories to *St. Nicholas* yet. It is too soon. You must learn the trade first and nobody can do that without a long and diligent apprenticeship—not anything short of ten years. Write the stories, write lots and lots of them for practice, and when the Literary League gets together again we'll examine into your progress and take note of such improvements as we find.

We have a very nice thoughtful little cat and it catches snakes and brings them into the house for us to play with.

3:30 P.M.—time to get up—SLC—who misses you, dear.

Not a word about the honorable mention, and I had been so proud of it!

At the time I was, of course, bitterly disappointed, but his words did me more good than any amount of praise would have done, for they impressed themselves upon my mind with all the force he meant them to have and I never forgot them. I took them to my heart and followed their advice and waited much more than the prescribed ten years before I sent out a story again!

17

Tammany and the Coal Bins

ONE OF THE FIRST SNAPSHOTS I ever possessed of Mark Twain was one that he gave me during my first Tuxedo visit. It had been taken years before when he was living in Florence and showed him with a lovely gray cat in his arms.

"That cat," he remarked, "tolerated me a little more kindly than any other of the species I've ever had. You know that's one of the reasons cats are so fascinating to me. You can never get close to them. They cuddle up to you and purr—like all women, when you stroke their heads, but they don't love you. They only tolerate—yes, that's the right word, tolerate. I think that's why I keep on having them about. I'm always hopeful I can break one down and get a spark of affection out of it. If I keep at it long enough I may succeed. So far all I've gotten is condescension. I wouldn't like it from a human, but it's rather amusing from a cat."

At this point he started to stride up and down the porch and I knew I was going to hear more on the subject. Whenever

Mr. Clemens got intensely interested in anything, he began striding around the room restlessly, just as he did when he was dictating his stories. As he enlarged upon his topic, it would nearly always develop into a monologue, and his listeners would hardly dare move for fear of breaking the spell.

This time, with the lovely garden of his Tuxedo home for a stage setting and the towering mountains for a background, he held forth.

"I like cats. They are the one animal that is completely independent. They never exhibit their feelings and there is an innate dignity about them that I particularly admire. It is such a contrast to me. I always wanted to be inscrutable and could never quite manage it. Any cat could give me cards and spades on that score and still come off the victor."

His face was unsmiling as he talked.

"Beneath their softness is always lurking their savage ancestry, just as their claws are hidden in their feet. Those innocent little paws, yet look what they can do to you when they make up their mind to it! I always treat cats with respect. It pays to be respectful to someone that has the power to hurt you—that is, unless you're a good distance away, where it's quite safe to let loose."

He made one or two more rapid turns before he came back to where I was sitting, with the snapshot still in my hands. He looked at it over my shoulder. I realized the dissertation was finished and began to murmur something about cats always finding their way home.

"You little innocent," he chuckled, peering down at me from under his heavy eyebrows. "I suppose you think they come back because they love you."

I nodded violently.

"Disabuse your mind on that subject, here and now. They

come back for their nice saucers of milk, bits of liver and helpings of fish. That's the only masculine trait in their nature. They do come to eat. But if they met someone on the way that could do better by them so far as their daily menu is concerned, they'd stay right there. You can take that from one who knows as gospel truth. In fact, more than gospel— because I never was quite sure about the veracity of that!"

Just at this point Mr. Clemens was called to the telephone to speak to Colonel Harvey. When he returned I had discovered that a brand new flower had presented itself in the nasturtium bed, so the conversation took a different turn.

Cats were more or less always mixed up with my friendship for Mr. Clemens from those Tuxedo days. I had hardly returned from my last visit there when Mr. Clemens wrote that a little cat had strayed onto their porch and was proving the point he had made in his talk, for after its first meal it had definitely adopted them. And in his last letter from Tuxedo he spoke of its bringing snakes for them to play with.

Hearing this, I was rather glad that the cat had arrived after my departure. If there was anything in the world I was afraid of, it was a snake. Once when on one of our walks we had seen a long green streak sliding through the grass, I had screamed and covered my face with my hands. Mr. Clemens watched the reptile disappear before he said, "Well, well, that's the Eve in you coming out! But you can stop being an ostrich now, the snake has gone."

Remembering this, I wasn't quite sure whether the little cat had actually caught the snakes or Mr. Clemens was trying to tease me by reminding me of the day I had imitated an ostrich. Apparently, though, he was quite serious and the new addition to the household was reverting to type by predatory hunting, for he had already mentioned its catching a bird, and in another letter he spoke of its hunting insects. The little cat continually thrust its personality into the pages of Mr. Clemens' letters.

By this time my curiosity to see the little cat had mounted almost to a fever pitch. Needless to say, I was glad to hear that it was going to be brought back to New York so I could make its acquaintance. It rather worried me that all this time it had been unnamed, but Mr. Clemens had said he wanted to find just the right name for it. I spent a long time making out a list of names that I thought would be "fetching," to borrow one of Mr. Clemens' favorite words, and when I went in to visit him at Fifth Avenue for the first time, I took the list with me.

So eager was I to see the "little cat" that the greetings were hardly over before I asked for it and produced my list. Mr. Clemens took it with his never-failing courtesy, and after reading it carefully, put it safely in his pocket.

"They're good names and we will use them for whatever other pets we may have. Unfortunately, they're too late for the little cat. She's already christened. It didn't take me long to find a name for her once we'd reached New York. When I discovered she is a terrible scrapper and couldn't be kept in nights, I knew the right and appropriate name for her was 'Tammany.' "

I was properly introduced to Tammany then and there, and afterward the little cat, who was really grown up before I made her acquaintance, was one of the outstanding features of No. 21. She was a great pet and everyone made much of her—particularly Mr. Clemens.

A very amusing incident, of which Tammany was the central pivot, happened later that winter. I had been unable to come in for a visit for several weeks as I had had bronchitis.

When, having got over it, I finally arrived at No. 21, Mr. Clemens announced he had a surprise for me. I was all agog! He was always giving me presents, and I always loved them; so I told him I could hardly wait to see what the surprise was.

"Hardly wait! You little rat! I've waited almost three weeks to tell you and it's been the most difficult waiting. Twice I had to tear up letters I'd written you because I'd given the surprise away in them, and I wanted to see your face when you knew! Run along with Catherine and do your unpacking and then come down to the billiard room."

I went reluctantly with the maid and hurried up the bags as quickly as possible. I changed my dark dress for a white one, as I always did when I arrived, for Mr. Clemens still liked me to wear the white he loved. I almost slid down the stairs and ran right into Mr. Clemens, who was waiting for me at the entrance to the billiard room. He caught me so that I didn't lose my balance and told me to shut my eyes. Once I had done so, he led me into the billiard room and over toward the window seat at the far end. Then he said, "Now—you can look!"

I opened my eyes, and there was Tammany with four of the most adorable kittens I had ever seen. I dropped to the floor beside the window seat and gathered two of the little bunches of fur into my arms.

"She had them down cellar," Mr. Clemens told me, "and she keeps them there. She's a very jealous and secretive mother. It took Claude a long time to find them. This is their first trip upstairs. I've been saving it till you came. It was worth waiting to see the look on your face. I knew it would be. Surprises fall flat usually, but this one was a huge success. Tammany and I, working together, are invincible, I do believe that."

"Oh, look!" I exclaimed, interrupting, for there was Tammany with one of the kittens in her mouth making for the door.

"She'll take it back down cellar," Mr. Clemens explained, "and then return for the others. You just watch."

Sure enough, that's just what that "wise and sagacious" cat did. She made three trips and then sat and cried so pathetically that I had to let her take the last remaining fluff-ball from my lap.

"Never mind," Mr. Clemens comforted. "We'll play billiards and after lunch go down and fetch them up again."

All of which is only a prelude to other amusing happenings. That afternoon, true to his word, Mr. Clemens took me down to the cellar to find the kittens. Tammany had evidently suspected our intentions, for she had hidden them in the coalbin. Nothing daunted, Mr. Clemens and I scrambled over the shifting coals with utter disregard of our clothes.

We had just succeeded in capturing the last kitten when the butler arrived to announce that my mother and a young lady were waiting upstairs. Mr. Clemens and I had both forgotten that Mother was bringing the daughter of one of my grandfather's most important clients to tea that afternoon. The young girl, only in New York for the day, was from the South and had always longed to meet Mark Twain. When Mother had told him so, he had said with his usual graciousness to bring her along that afternoon.

"We'll be right up," Mr. Clemens told Claude and then, turning to me, said, "Come along, and don't lose those kittens. I couldn't go delving into those bins again, even for you, dear heart. Not at my age!"

We went upstairs and paused for a minute in front of the long mirror in the hall. For the first time we caught a full view of ourselves. The light in the cellar had been dim, but here it was only too revealing. Mr. Clemens had a black smudge across his forehead and chin. I was similarly decorated, only in my case it was mostly on the nose. Our white clothes were a perfect background for long streaks of coal dust, and we each held in our hands squirming kittens whose every move rubbed off a little more black on us.

We looked at each other in despair. From the living room we could hear the gentle murmur of voices. There wasn't time to change. We both knew Mother and the Southern girl had trains to catch.

Finally a little mischevious twinkle appear in Mr. Clemens eyes. He put his finger to his mouth and then, after having assured my silence, handed me his two kittens and ran his fingers through his hair. It had become flattened during the cellar exploration, and this was one of his most characteristic mannerisms when he wanted to fluff it up. But he wasn't as successful as usual, for quite a bit of the dirt on his hands was transferred to his hair during the process.

Then he solemnly winked at me, like a naughty little boy who knows he's about to do something he shouldn't and with his head thrown back like a general and his arm around my shoulder, we marched into the living room. He had quite forgotten that I had four wriggling kittens in my arms. We made quite a procession, with Tammany leading the way!

Mother took one look at us and gasped. The young lady, a typical Southern belle, who looked as though she had just stepped out of the show window of a Fifth Avenue store, couldn't quite believe her eyes. Mother told me afterward that the Southern lass had spent hours on her toilette, making ready for the call. Her immaculate tan dress, with shoes, stockings, and gloves to match, was a terrific contrast to the mussed and dirty appearance Mr. Clemens and I presented.

She had come to meet a famous author and found what looked to be a miner coming out of the mine after a hard day's work, literally surrounded by cats—the excitement had made me forget the kittens and I had dropped them. They were crawling over the floor while Tammany, rather pleased at the attention her offspring were receiving, purred loudly.

"Dorothy!" My Mother's horrified exclamation was the first word that was spoken.

Before Mother could say anything more, Mr. Clemens stepped forward. "A little dirt doesn't hurt anyone. Please don't make Dorothy change her dress. She had such a good time playing with Tammany and the kittens. I always feel sorry for clean children. They look as though they never have a good time. Now, anyone could tell after one glance at Dorothy and me, we've been thoroughly enjoying ourselves."

Over Mother's shoulder he winked at me, and I knew he'd composed his speech that brief moment we had stood in front of the mirror before our entrance. After that there was nothing Mother could say. She shook hands with Mr. Clemens and presented him to her visitor who put her beautiful gloved hand into Mr. Clemens' without a thought of the smudges it would receive.

Mr. Clemens took out his handkerchief and wiped off most of his smudges while Mother did the same for me, and before we knew it the Southern belle was down on the floor acquiring a little dirt of her own from the kittens.

She didn't want Mr. Clemens to feel sorry for her!

18

No. 21 Fifth Avenue: "Was It Heaven? or Hell?"

IT WAS THE END of October before Mark Twain returned to New York. I was very excited when I received a telephone call the day he arrived at No. 21 Fifth Avenue. He wanted to know when I could come in.

I didn't lose much time setting a date, and it was arranged that I should go in on Friday afternoon and stay until Monday morning. This meant that I would miss Saturday morning's school and Monday's, but as it was a special occasion, even the Principal made the way easy for me to secure the necessary permission.

I was all agog. I had missed my "elderly friend" more than I would have believed possible. Not only had I missed him and the good times he had given me, but I also missed the grown-up feeling I had when I was with him, and the continual excitement.

Too, there were no rules for little girls at Mark Twain's house. And that wasn't the least of its charms.

No. 21 Fifth Avenue: "Was It Heaven? or Hell?"

The sun was shining brightly when Mother and I got out
of the cab in front of Mr. Clemens' house on the corner of
Tenth Street and Fifth Avenue. It seems a curious thing, but
in all the time I spent with Mr. Clemens, I can never remember
anything but sunshine, both withindoors and without. Even
in Tuxedo, and later in Redding which was noted for its
storms, the weather stayed clear and lovely the entire length
of my visits—a fact so unusual that Mr. Clemens remarked
upon it himself. Only he said, "You bring sunshine with you,
Dorothy."

The fact remains that I always associate him with brightness
and cheer. The sun shining on his bright hair, outlining his
figure as he walked, bringing out the lines life had destined
him to wear—always the sunlight illuminating the days I
spent with him.

So I wasn't surprised that the sun was flooding Fifth Avenue
with its brilliance as I arrived at Mark Twain's house. It was
the old brownstone-front type, with a long flight of steps leading from the sidewalk up to its front door. The house, itself,
was a large one—four-storied, with a somewhat ecclesiastical
appearance. The windows were set in with a stony tracery of
churchlike carving which, even to the most casual observer,
stamped it as having been at one time connected with a church.
As a matter of fact, it had originally been a church property,
probably a parish house or parsonage. But Mr. Clemens said
he would never hold that against it!

Mr. William Lyon Phelps, when showing pictures of the
house at the Mark Twain centenary dinner, remarked on its
ecclesiastical front and said it was probably the nearest to a
church Mark ever got in his later years.

At any rate, its churchly antecedents had left large, richly
ornamented windows and on the side street a beautiful bay

115

window, which had a wonderful view up the Avenue, where Mr. Clemens loved to sit and watch the crowds. The room with the bay window was the living room.

When one entered the house, one faced the stairs that led to the upper regions. There was a small hall with the long mirror and hatrack that in those days was an essential part of any home. On the left was the living room, a long, somewhat narrow room which not only had the bay window but also possessed two very long windows directly on Fifth Avenue itself. At the opposite end were the massive folding doors that opened into the dining room, which was always resplendent with old mahogany and gleaming silver on the sideboard.

In the living room, close by the bay window, was the stuffed arm chair with the high back in which Mark Twain liked best to sit. When he reclined himself in it, with his meerschaum pipe held lovingly in his hand and a book on his knees, he presented a picture that could have been labeled "Comfort and content."

It was here that he was waiting for me. And this time I appreciated the honor, for it was only a little past eleven, and hadn't he said in his last letter from Tuxedo, "three-thirty P. M., time to get up." So when I saw him standing in the doorway as Claude opened the front door, I was properly thrilled and flew in to greet him. In fact, I was so enthusiastic that I almost knocked him over with the sheer force of my arrival.

Mother stayed for a few minutes and then said good-by and went off, promising to come for me at eleven o'clock on Monday. Catherine had already whisked my bag up to the room that was to be mine on the third floor—really the fourth, if one counted the basement, but as I never did it always remained the third floor to me.

As soon as the first enthusiasm of my arrival had worn off and I had been introduced to Tammany, Mr. Clemens took me upstairs to see "my" room, which was in the front of the house. His secretary had the room next to mine, so she could more or less keep an eye on me. My bags were unpacked and everything was in order, from the dish of fruit on the table at the bedside to the white dresses hung in the closet.

I was too happy over seeing him again to want to waste any time changing my clothes, so after a hasty look around we went downstairs again and Mr. Clemens showed me the second floor. In the front, directly under my room, his daughter, Clara Clemens, had her rooms. She was away on a concert tour so I didn't meet her on this visit, but I saw her bedroom and sitting room with its grand piano. Then I was taken to see the room in the middle of the floor which was his own.

It was a large, square room, and a good thing that it was, for Mark Twain's bed needed a room of grand proportions. It was a massive thing of mahogany with four thick pillars to mark the corners, which were richly carved. I had never seen anything quite like it except in palaces abroad, and remarked naïvely that I didn't know anyone really slept in beds like that!

"Well, I do," said Mr. Clemens. "Not very well, sometimes, I must admit, but I can't blame that on the bed. It's a nice bed, Dorothy, and I'm fond of it. You will see how well I look in it when you come to say 'good morning.' "

"It's a King's bed!" I exclaimed.

"Certainly," he agreed instantly. "That's why I've got it."

I made a little curtsy. As I did so I looked at the table along-side the bed that was piled high with books and papers, and took a casual glance at the chairs and bureau that, in contrast to the magnificent bed, seemed very unimportant. Then Mr. Clemens said, "And now I will show you my favorite room in this house."

I expected as we walked down the hall, hand in hand, that we were going to a library. Although I wasn't right I was not entirely wrong, for the room into which he led me had a built-in bookcase and hundreds of books. Still, it wasn't a library. It was a billiard room, entirely dominated by a large billiard table that had been presented to Mark Twain by his friend, H. H. Rogers.

This room was at the back of the house and at the very end of it were the built-in bookcases. There was a window seat which ran the entire width of the room across the window and at the bottom of the bookcases, which spilled over on the sides too, so that the seat ran the length of the walls also. The windows were in the center of the back part of the room, with the books on either side of it. There were other windows on the Tenth Street side of the house, so that the room was always light and airy.

One end of it, the end near the door by which we entered, was entirely given up to the billiard table's appendages—the rack for the cues, and the marker that was strung across from wall to well, upon which Mr. Clemens piled up his scores with great glee.

When I saw the billiard table, I clapped my hands. "Oh, you've got a billiard room! Can I play with you?"

Mr. Clemens stepped back a little and surveyed me. "Can you play with me?" he repeated; then with an entirely different inflection, "*Can* you play billiards?"

"Oh, yes, we've always had a billiard table and I often play. I am not very good at it, but I love it."

Mr. Clemens was more excited about my being able to play his favorite game than I had been over the discovery of the billiard table. "That's what I like about you, Dorothy," he

This photograph of us, taken on the side porch of Mark Twain's home in Tuxedo Park, was his favorite.

One of my endeavors ——— Mark Twain was a very photogenic figure.

exclaimed. "You're so full of surprises. I never know what's coming next and I revel in the uncertainty."

Meanwhile, he was busy at the cue rack, procuring one that wouldn't be too heavy for me to use. When he finally found one, he carefully chalked the end of it and handed it to me. Then he put the balls on the table and said, "Go ahead dear, and show me what you can do."

I must have performed not too discreditably, for he called for his secretary to come in and see how well I held my cue. After that, whenever anyone came in, he lost no time in getting up a game to exhibit my billiard-playing ability, and he inevitably commented on the progress I was making.

That first day in New York he lost no time in initiating me into a new form of billiards which he had just discovered himself, "Cowboy Pool." It was particularly well adapted for a pastime as it didn't require the skill necessary for billiards, so we had great fun with it.

So far as I was concerned, Cowboy Pool was such a success that whenever Mark Twain asked, "What would you like to do now?" I immediately voted for the new game. This was a ballot after his own heart. The billiard room was the center of life in the old mansion. Here Mark Twain was at his happiest, enjoying himself, and he would never stop playing as long as he had an opponent. Sometimes, even when he hadn't one, he would amuse himself knocking the balls around, "for practice."

He spent quite a bit of time giving me pointers and easily won every game we played, which, as he said, "Is really lots of fun because you're so very nice about losing and you can always console yourself with the thought that you're very young, dear, and when you get to be my age you can easily beat me."

I was having such a good time that I quite forgot that in our house the billiard table was never used on Sunday. My grandparents were Scotch Presbyterians of the old school who strongly disapproved of playing games on the Lord's Day—or even the piano, for that matter. My mother was much more liberal in her views but conformed to her parents' way of thinking.

At Mark Twain's I didn't even realize that it was Sunday. There was no mention of church, and no difference made in the day, so I forgot its significance and enjoyed my game of pool just as much as though it weren't the Sabbath.

But when I returned home and was recounting the good times I had had, I quite innocently mentioned, "We played billiards all the time!" I remembered the family inhibitions as I saw my grandfather's face change its expression and heard his voice asking if I had played on Sunday. I replied truthfully that I had, and after expressing his views on the subject, Grandfather asked me to promise not to do so again. Seeing how upset he was over it, I did so readily enough, but with a certain regret that the good times would be curtailed even so much, and a little wonder about how I was going to break the news to SLC.

However, there was no choice in the matter. The very next time I visited Mr. Clemens, when Sunday arrived, I announced regretfully that I couldn't play pool. I was a little worried for fear SLC would be angry, and very much relieved to discover he was only puzzled.

"Forever why not'?' he asked, so surprised that he actually took his big black cigar out of his mouth.

I caught my breath. I hated so to disappoint him in anything, and, too, I was being deprived of so much pleasure myself. I hesitated, then finally blurted out the truth.

"Because it's Sunday and my Grandfather doesn't approve of playing games on Sunday."

Mark Twain put his cigar back in the corner of his mouth. He took a long comforting pull at it and sent a cloud of smoke up toward the ceiling before he replied. "Very well, then, we shan't go to the devil today."

I laughed because the idea of his going to the devil seemed so incongruous. "You couldn't anyway," I exclaimed. "You'd have to wear red and you never wear anything but white, so you've got to go to Heaven."

"Out of the mouths of . . . ." he began and then broke off suddenly and drawled slowly. "I will read you a story of mine instead of playing pool. Do you think that will be all right?"

I nodded enthusiastically.

"Well, I'm not so sure, but we've got to take a chance now and then—even on Sunday."

We had a lovely day, despite the lack of billiards. He read to me a short story entitled, "Heaven or Hell," which he said seemed "appropriate." It was a very moving tale about someone who lied to save another person pain, and ended up with the question of the reward, "Was it Heaven—or Hell?"

I unreservedly voted for heaven and so did Mr. Clemens. That being settled, we went for a drive on Fifth Avenue, and by the time we had arrived back at No. 21 and had tea, Mother was there to take me home.

I had thought Mr. Clemens had forgotten all about the no-playing-games-on-Sunday pronouncement. But I discovered just as I was leaving that it was still very much on his mind, for he looked at Mother and said to her in his dry, inimitable way, "I'm quite sure I did nothing today to corrupt Dorothy's morals. For the first time in my life I've had a perfectly religious day. I've neither played cards, billiards, nor sworn, and do you know," he paused impressively and then continued, "I don't think I feel a bit the worse for it."

Though his speech was grave and his mouth unsmiling, by the time he had finished there was a twinkle in his eye, and both Mother and I were laughing so gaily he had to join in.

19

Billiards with Albert Bigelow Paine

I EXPECT I MUST HAVE BEEN a source of constant amusement to Mr. Clemens. I had been brought up in a very narrow, old-fashioned way which was such a complete contrast to Mark Twain's broad and generous outlook on life that it must have often tickled him and aroused his keen sense of humor. But if it did, he was too much the gentleman ever to let me see it. Instead, he would tell me I reminded him of his own little girls, and each time he spoke of me in connection with his other children, I felt happier than ever.

His daughter Jean I never saw. She was away, ill, at a sanatorium when I visited him in New York and Redding; but during my second stay at No. 21, I did meet his daughter Clara.

To me Clara Clemens seemed like a beautiful goddess, enveloped in rosy clouds, who graciously extended the aura of her glamour as a singer and the sweetness of her personality to the little girl who was her father's friend.

"This is Dorothy that I've written you about," Mr. Clemens

said when he introduced me to her. Clara immediately made me feel that she was glad to see me, and took me into her own room to show me some masks that she had made for a party, and asked me if I would like to have them. They were perfectly fascinating papier-mâché faces, and, of course, I was delighted at the prospect of having them for my own. Miss Clemens said she would have them packed and sent to me.

I had heard from Mr. Clemens that Clara was a singer, so I looked longingly toward the grand piano, hoping that I might perhaps hear her sing. I might have, but at that moment a caller was announced, and Miss Clemens had to go downstairs. I returned to the billiard room where Mark Twain was waiting impatiently.

Miss Clemens had a sweet Madonnalike face, with dark hair and eyes. The very fact that she was a singer made me look up to her with the greatest awe and admiration.

The mornings she spent singing in her own apartment, going over the songs that she intended using in her concerts. She always had her doors closed so that the music wouldn't interfere with her father's genius, which was burning in a different way.

Mark Twain's routine in New York was quite different than it had been in Tuxedo. At No. 21 he would lie in bed until ten or half past and read the papers and his mail. Then he would work from eleven until one, so that I never saw him in the morning unless his door was open when I came downstairs and he waved a "good morning" to me as I passed by.

He would be half-sitting, half-reclining in his massive bed, propped up by numerous pillows, and so surrounded with smoke from the black cigar or pipe that sometimes it was hard to distinguish him through the clouds that enveloped him. In his hand would be his fountain pen and on his lap a pad on which he wrote busily.

I knew that nothing must happen to disturb him, so I would tiptoe by the door on my way to the billiard room. Sometimes he would pause long enough to call out, "Hello, Dorothy, I'll be along presently"; other times he would be so intent on what he was doing that he wouldn't see me at all. Generally the door would be closed, until finally he appeared ready for the day's activities.

From my room upstairs I could always hear the faint sounds of music when Clara Clemens was singing. At the first note I would creep softly down and sit on the stairway at a point which brought me almost level with the top of her door. I would lean my head on the bannister and become entirely absorbed in the lovely tones of Miss Clemens' voice.

One morning I was listening so intently that I didn't hear Mark Twain's door open. My first knowledge I had of his presence in the hall was when I heard his startled voice asking, "What in the world are you doing there?"

I looked down through the railing and saw my friend peering up at me. His bushy eyebrows had shot up to an astonished angle and given his face a most quizzical expression. "Sh," I whispered, "I'm listening."

"To what?" Mr. Clemens said. There was ground for his question, for almost simultaneously with his appearance in the hall, the music had ceased.

I explained. "Miss Clemens was singing and I just had to listen. I often do. I didn't think she'd mind. I do wish I could sing like that some day." I was very serious. I had a real envy of Miss Clemens' ability.

Mark Twain's eyebrows no longer looked astonished. They drew together in a way I had never seen before. He shook his head until his white hair swayed back and forth as though he were out in a wind.

"You little rascal!" he said, "I won't accept your resignation from the Authors' League at this point. It would be all wrong and I couldn't think of allowing it. You can't change a career as easily as you change your mind, even if you are feminine!" He struck his hand down hard on the bannister to emphasize his words.

I thought he was really cross with me and hastily protested, "Oh, I haven't changed my mind. I do want to be an author, but I thought I might do both."

"To do one thing well will take all your time. I don't know anything about your voice but I am sure you can write so you'd better stick to that."

"Oh, I will, I will!" I promised. "Only you said drawing was good training for the mind and geometry, and that they would help me to be an author—so I didn't see why singing. . . ."

"It's different, dear. You must have a goal to make and follow the path directly to it. You can do lots of things to help you towards it, but you can't have two goals. You can't be a writer and a singer. They're different aims and to achieve a goal one must devote every atom of his being to it and not split up one's energies going after something else. Besides," he drew himself up until I could have touched his hair, "I can't teach you singing." There was a wistful quality in his voice that made me regret I had ever wanted to sing.

I ran down the stairs and held out my hand to him. "I'd rather be an author like you than anything in the whole world," I whispered, my head against his arm.

"Then that's settled!" he exclaimed happily as his eyebrows

relaxed into their normal position. He patted my head and then said, "The singing seems to be over for the day. It's too near lunch time for us to do a story so I think we'd better play billiards."

And we went down the hall to the billiard room, arm in arm, to find Tammany curled up on the table with her head on Mr. Clemens' best white ball, purring as contentedly as though it had been made of down instead of ivory.

Mr. Clemens must have told his daughter about her unseen audience, because after that morning, whenever Miss Clemens sang, the door was left a little ajar. Then I could hear perfectly, and I was very grateful, although I never quite had the courage to tell the object of my admiration.

Clara Clemens was always sweet to me and did a great deal to make my visits to No. 21 happy ones. She had to be away a great deal on her concert tours, and it was a real cause for rejoicing on all sides whenever she was at home.

At No. 21, I was constantly seeing celebrities. There wasn't a day that passed that didn't have some interesting event connected with it.

One day Mr. Clemens introduced me to a tall, thin man, saying with great pride, "This is my biographer, Albert Bigelow Paine, Dorothy."

As I shook hands with Mr. Paine, I regarded him intently, for I wasn't quite sure just what a biographer was and I hoped that he would say or do something to enlighten me. I guessed that a biographer must be something terribly important, and my curiosity mounted to a fever pitch. Mr. Paine, not knowing this, began telling me that he had often heard Mr. Clemens speak of me and went on to say how glad he was to meet me at last. Then he asked how I liked visiting at Mark Twain's.

I promptly replied, "I like it best of anything I've done yet."
Mr. Clemens was very much amused. "You notice the reservation, of course, Paine," he remarked *sotto voce*.

I decided that the way things were going I would never get to find out what a biographer was, so I took my courage in both hands and seized the first opportunity to ask Mr. Paine, himself. Mr. Clemens turned his back on us, and I could see his shoulders move. Mr. Paine was very kind. He carefully explained that a biographer was a person who writes the life of another person and that he was writing the life of Mark Twain.

"Oh," I exclaimed, a trifle disappointed that the explanation was so simple. "I didn't know writing a life of someone would have such a long name."

By now Mr. Clemens had turned around and come back to where we were standing. He put one arm around me and laid his other hand on Mr. Paine's shoulder. "It deserves a long name, Dorothy. It's a long job—especially such a full life as mine. I'm very lucky to have such an able writer to give an account of me."

After that introduction I saw a great deal of Mr. Paine, for he was often at the house.

Another very frequent guest at No. 21 was Martin Littleton, who even then was established as one of the most famous criminal lawyers of his day. He and his wife lived in an apartment house on the opposite side of Fifth Avenue, and Mr. Littleton often used to stroll over in the evening for a game of pool with Mark Twain. He would say that it was the relaxation and fun of playing with Mr. Clemens that enabled him to face the long days in court.

Anxious as Mr. Clemens was to know what was going on at his interesting trials, he got no satisfaction from Mr. Littleton. Mr. Littleton refused to be drawn out, and despite the good-natured chaffing on the subject from Mark Twain and the sly casts for information, Mr. Littleton would only say, "We are going to win." Then he would turn to the subject— billiards—in the manner that was daily adding to his fame in the courtroom.

Mr. and Mrs. Littleton were often invited to dinner, and Mrs. Littleton would talk to me while the men played pool. Several times she took Mr. Clemens and me for afternoon drives up Fifth Avenue, behind the beautiful pair of sorrel horses the Littletons had at that time.

Mr. Littleton wasn't particularly interested in little girls. His attention was entirely engrossed in the game he was playing. I would take my place on the cushioned seat that ran around the three walls of the room and watch the game. Mr. Clemens always called my attention to any plays of special interest and made comments to me on the game as it went along. But so far as Mr. Littleton was concerned, I might have been part of the furniture, and I think he felt the "time out" that Mr. Clemens took to explain things to me was wasted.

But Mr. Paine, whenever he happened to be playing with them, would come and sit beside me and tell me about his own daughters in so interesting a fashion that I was always sorry when it came time for him to play again.

Every time Mr. Clemens added markers to his own score, he would chuckle and wink at me behind Mr. Littleton's back and throw out his shoulders, so that I knew without words that he was saying, "See what I can do!" And the more markers he strung up for himself, the more pleased he would look.

There were other visitors at No. 21. Colonel Harvey came, and it was always a pleasure to see him again. His keen, alert eyes behind the heavy-rimmed spectacles he affected never missed anything; but like Mr. Clemens' own, they were always kindly, and he, too, liked little girls.

Then there was the Reverend Joseph Twichell, who used to come to see his old boyhood friend—but not often, because he lived far away from New York. His visits were rare enough to be events, and it always gave Mr. Clemens much pleasure to welcome Joe.

When he arrived there would be a clang of the front door—loud enough for us to hear it up in the billiard room; then a voice would waft up the stairs, "Hello, Sam!" Mr. Clemens would put down his cue and walk out into the hall, a good bit faster than his ordinary gait, and lean over the balustrade and call back, "Hello, Joe. Come on up!"

The Reverend Twichell would come puffing up the stairs until he reached the hall. Then he would put his hands on Mr. Clemens' shoulders and say, "Well, well, Sam, it is good to see you again."

Together they would come into the billiard room and then the reminiscences would fly back and forth quicker than a shuttlecock.

It was fun listening to them but it always aroused a little envy, too, because Mr. Clemens would invariably lean over in my direction and say, "It's too bad you didn't know us in those days, Dorothy," and the more I heard this, the more sure I was that he was right.

There were other famous visitors who were constantly in the house, and whom I grew to know. Margaret Illington and Daniel Frohman, to whom she was married at the time, came, as did H. H. Rogers, David Munro, Frederick A. Duneka of Harper and Brothers, and still more whose names I didn't remember. All gathered around Mark Twain very much as courtiers congregate about their king.

Sometimes when I was there Clara Clemens would have luncheons and then the guests would be singers and the table would revolve around musical matters. Even then Mr. Clemens could hold his own as though it had been of books.

Once the guest of honor was Miss Geraldine Farrar and I couldn't eat my luncheon at all, I was so fascinated by her beauty and personality. I thought I had never seen anything so dazzling as the flash of her white teeth as she smiled.

Despite my youth, Mr. Clemens always insisted that I come to the table, and even when he gave a formal dinner, I still retained my seat beside him. I've often wished that I had been older and been able to take stenographic notes of the conversations; I'm sure there would have been material for several books, had I been able to retain them clearly in my mind.

20

Mussed Braids at the Pleiades Club

DURING THE CHRISTMAS VACATION I was able to stay a longer time than two days, so Mark Twain arranged for me to come in to No. 21 for a week. He wrote in his letter, "I will be up and waiting for you when you come."

This—since I arrived at eleven—was really something for him to do, and now that I knew more about his habits I appreciated the effort he was making for me.

As soon as Claude opened the door, I would fly in and, emulating Reverend Twichell, call out, "Hello, SLC!" Then the beloved white head would pop out from between the living room curtains, and the slow drawl reach my ears, "Hello, Dorothy, I am glad you've come." And we would go up to the billiard room, which was so steeped in its owner's charm that it had acquired an attraction of its own.

The Christmas visit was seven days of unmitigated joy. There was never a minute of the time that wasn't fully occupied. The Authors' League was not neglected, nor were Tammany, the billiards, or any of the other things that had been so much fun at Tuxedo. We still had the daily drives, only now instead of being in the open victoria along woodsy roads, we drove up Fifth Avenue in a closed brougham drawn by a pair of tan horses that threw their heads back and snorted with glee when they reached the Park, which I supposed represented the country to them.

Often on the way up the Avenue, Mark Twain would get out of the carriage and walk a way, while he smoked the heavy black cigars he enjoyed so much. He liked strong tobacco and smoked the cheapest brands because they were more biting. I would stay in the carriage, and as he was a brisk walker, he easily caught up with us. In fact, the carriage had to proceed so slowly through the traffic that before we knew it we would see him standing on the corner waving his cigar as a signal for us to stop and pick him up.

Once he had resumed his place by my side, he would begin to tell me the adventures he had had during his walk. It was very rare when he returned without at least one amusing incident to relate. Once it was an encounter with a woman who, not lacking in temerity, rushed up to him with the question. "Are you Mark Twain?" When he politely admitted he was, she tried to press him further, saying she wanted to be quite sure because he certainly didn't look like the pictures she'd seen of Mark Twain.

"What do you think of that?" Mr. Clemens asked, "trying to tell me I wasn't myself. There are some people in the world who, if you told them the sun was shining, would swear it was the moon, just to be different, even though they knew it was the sun all the time. Aren't you glad I'm not like that, Dorothy? Just think how awful it would be if I went around declaring I wasn't Mark Twain. Think what the world would lose!"

Another time he came back to the carriage shaking with laughter.

"Oh, what's happened this time?" I asked as he pulled the door shut behind him and relaxed into his seat.

In reply he pointed out of the carriage window toward a little boy who was walking up the Avenue with a woman, obviously his mother.

"Do you see that child?" Mark Twain asked. "The little boy attached to the hand of the woman in blue?"

I leaned forward eagerly. "Oh, yes!"

"Well," said SLC, "I just heard him exclaim as I walked by, 'Look, Mama—there goes the daddy of Phoebe Snow!'"

When the peal of laughter he evidently expected from me didn't come, he peered down and asked. "Don't you think that's funny?"

I hesitated and then admitted the truth. "I don't know who Phoebe Snow is."

"Heavens, child, don't you read advertisements? No wonder you didn't laugh with me! Phoebe Snow is a well known advertisement for a railroad, 'A young lady in white who rides the Road of Anthracite,' and remains immaculately clean. As Phoebe always wears white, my white suit brought me the credit of having given her birth."

Now I did indeed share the joke with him.

Often people stopped Mark Twain on the street, just for the pleasure of shaking hands with him. Mr. Clemens was always gracious to his admirers. In fact, he enjoyed the attention they paid him, and if he had had to return to the carriage without an adventure or a compliment of some sort to report, he would have felt very disappointed. There never was a man who appreciated his "public" and his popularity more than Mark Twain.

Usually, whenever I spent the week end with him, he planned something special for Saturday afternoon—either a matinee or a visit to a museum or an art gallery. Once he had planned to take me to the police parade, but unluckily that week end I had an attack of bronchitis and couldn't come in. So instead he sent me a picture of himself in the grandstand next to the mayor and told me of the treat I had missed. He said he had had to take someone else in my place and he had missed me.

I felt very badly, for it would have been wonderful to have seen the parade under such circumstances. When the next week I was still sick and cheated of being with him again, I wrote him saying how badly I felt not to see him again and to have to miss such a grand good time. He promptly replied, by way of consolation, that so far as the theater was concerned, I hadn't missed much. "I didn't like the matinee. It was too frivolous and vaudevillish, and too much ballet and clothes and foolish songs."

He was a stickler for good taste in the theater. During Christmas week he took me to see a mild little comedy, and though it was not at all risqué, he was quite shocked over it and greatly regretted having taken me, despite the fact that I had enjoyed it tremendously.

He always took a box, and it was lots of fun to see every neck in the audience craning toward it once the news had circulated about that Mark Twain was in the theater.

On December 22 the Pleiades Club was giving a dinner in honor of Mark Twain. They had special Sunday night dinners at the Hotel Brevoort and had been trying for a long time to induce Mr. Clemens to be a guest of honor. For some reason, he had steadily refused. This time, Mr. Ryan, who had been a fellow passenger on the *S. S. Minnetonka,* wouldn't give up hope that he might come. So the plans for the dinner in his honor went on, despite Mr. Clemens' continued refusal.

SLC said he appreciated the honor done him but was firm in his determination not to go. Even when Mr. Ryan and Mother stopped on their way to the dinner which was, being at the old Brevoort, almost next door, and did everything they could to persuade him, he still refused. He said he was very sorry but he had spoken a good deal of late and didn't feel he could do so just then, especially since he was scheduled for a speech at the Lotos Club dinner on January 11.

I was terribly disappointed. A card had come several weeks before from the executive committee of the Pleiades Club inviting "Mrs. Quick and Miss Dorothy Quick" to be guests of the Club at its dinner and entertainment in honor of Mark Twain. I had been all excited over it and had looked forward to being there more than I could have adequately expressed. And now I had to watch Mother and Mr. Ryan depart to the banquet I had been so eagerly anticipating!

I couldn't say anything. I tried to hide my bitter disappointment, but as the hour of the dinner grew nearer, I became more and more downcast. To have Mother so near and not to be with her—to miss the party was too much for my usual gay spirits!

Mr. Clemens, with his rare understanding, sensed immediately that something was wrong. "What's the matter, Dorothy?" he asked.

I shook my head. I didn't want him to guess how perilously close to tears I was.

"Did you want to go to the dinner?"

I nodded violently.

"Very much?"

My head must have resembled one of those German toys

that bob up and down with great momentum once they are started.

"Then we will go," he said, and immediately after giving me the glad tidings began roaring up the stairs telling his secretary to telephone to Mr. Ryan that we were coming to the dinner.

When his surprised secretary said, "I thought you'd decided not to go," Mr. Clemens replied, "Dorothy wants to go and I've just remembered there is something I'd like to talk about."

His secretary rushed to the telephone, and Mr. Clemens and I went off to our respective rooms to change our clothes.

Being Sunday night, Catherine, the maid who arranged my long braids, was out. With complete indifference, I did nothing to my hair, which was a little disarranged owing to my having played with Tammany who, as Mr. Clemens said, "Somehow, always seemed to disrupt one's personal appearance."

I put on my best dress unaided. Fortunately, it slipped on over my head and there were no buttons. My one idea was to get to the dinner, now that Mr. Clemens had decided to go. I didn't want anything to hold him up.

When we arrived at the Brevoort, Mother and Mr. Ryan were waiting for us. After one glance at me, Mother whisked me off to the dressing room, where she combed my unruly locks into order and redid the braids which, to my impatience, seemed to take forever. The time was made even longer by the fact that Mr. Clemens was kept waiting, for he wouldn't go in without me.

Finally I was all ready and we were escorted into the dining room and to our places at the speaker's table. I was seated next to Mr. Clemens, at his own request.

It was all very exciting and I had a wonderful time. They

had specially printed menus for the occasion, with a drawing of Mark Twain on the cover. It showed him with white hair swirling about his head in great waves and his eyebrows equally exaggerated; but the strong nose and eyes were true to life, as well as the drooping moustache and small chin which was, nevertheless, the firmest I have ever seen. It portrayed the low, turned down collar he invariably wore and was, according to Mr. Clemens, "A creditable likeness." He signed his menu card for me, "Mark Twain."

The menu card was a folder of three pages, and on the inside were sketches by various artists illustrating his books with a quotation from them. First was *Adam's Diary*, then, *Tom Sawyer, Innocents Abroad, Roughing It,* and *The Prince and The Pauper.* On the very back was the menu and over it a picture and quotation from *Joan of Arc* which pleased Mr. Clemens much more than the food, in which, truth to tell, we weren't interested at all, as we had had our early Sunday night supper at No. 21 long before we left.

Carter S. Cole was the toastmaster, and when he introduced Mark Twain he made a very flowery speech of thanks, "To the greatest humorist of our times for coming to our dinner."

Mark Twain got up immediately, looked around, and after bowing to his audience, smiled at me and said in the drawl which was so distinctively his own, "Dr. Cole, you shouldn't really thank me for coming. Any thanks for my presence here tonight should be given to Miss Dorothy Quick who brought me." There was a round of applause for me at that point, and after it had finally subsided, Mark Twain plunged into what he had wanted to say.

I couldn't tell you what it was. I was in too much of a flutter, thrilled to the very tips of my fingers. I only know that he told stories as he went along and that waves of laughter

138

swept over the audience; just as the moon influences the ocean, so Mark Twain held them in his hands and with no effort made the waters of their mirth ebb and flow as he pleased.

When he had finished speaking and bowing in response to the applause and had finally resumed his seat, Dr. Cole got up to announce the rest of the program. Much to my surprise, Mr. Clemens grasped me firmly by the hand and, whispering in my ear, "We're going now," pulled me up. Together we slipped out—not unnoticed, for Mr. Ryan came with us and helped Mr. Clemens into his coat and escorted us out to the waiting cab.

I hadn't had time to do more than wave in Mother's direction and say good-by to the very nice young lady across the narrow table who had been making a great fuss over me. As we drove off in the carriage, I said regretfully. "We didn't hear the young lady play the piano."

"Oh, I am so sorry," Mr. Clemens said. "If I'd realized that it was the same girl who talked to us during dinner who was going to play, I would have waited until she had finished. I wouldn't like to hurt her feelings, but it's high time for youngsters like us to be in bed."

And I never knew whether he left on my account or his own, because as he once pointed out, "Sitting at a banquet and listening to speeches is quite different than playing billiards and having a good time."

As the carriage rolled along I asked the question that had been in the back of my mind all evening. "However can you make up speeches so quickly?"

Mr. Clemens replied, "Oh, the idea has been simmering in my mind but I intended using it for another dinner that's coming along soon now. So you see, you little rascal, now that you wanted to go to this dinner, I've got to think out a new speech for the next one."

It was dark and I couldn't see whether his eyes were twinkling, which was my only way of knowing if he were making fun or being serious. If he weren't teasing, then I had made lots of trouble for him. I began to feel guilty but he immediately reassured me.

"Don't worry, dear. It won't matter. Once I get started words always bubble forth, so I'll find plenty to say at the next one. I'll tell them how a little girl's braids held up a large banquet. That will make them laugh!"

It made me laugh and by the time I had finished, the carriage had stopped before No. 21. As we went in, I said, "I wish I could hear you tell them."

"Very well, then you shall," he promised, and that night I went to sleep with another banquet to look forward to.

21

The Spirit of Christmas

THE DAY AFTER the Pleiades dinner was December 23, and Mother, who had stayed in town, came to No. 21 about four o'clock to have tea and take me home.

I could hardly wait for the ceremony of tea-drinking to be finished.

Upstairs in my room was a tiny box, all done up in white tissue paper and red ribbon. It had been wrapped and unwrapped many times by my eager fingers, for I wanted it to be "just right," as it was my Christmas present to SLC—the first time I had given him a present.

For weeks I had been planning my Christmas gift to him, and finally had selected a silver knife at Tiffany's and had it marked with his initials, "S. L. C."

Just as soon as tea was over, I asked to be excused and ran upstairs to fetch the precious box. I came down the stairs two at a time, I was so eager to "surprise" SLC.

Christmas, to me, was the most wonderful and exciting time

of the whole year. As a family, we had always made much of the day, and the joy of it was one that I was particularly anxious to share with my friend.

I had no idea that downstairs Mother and Mr. Clemens' secretary were waiting for the moment when I would present my gift, with very different feelings from mine. To them it was a very anxious moment, fraught with all sorts of ominous possibilities. Indeed, it might have ended the friendship that had grown to mean so much to Mark Twain and myself.

For years, ever since the death of Mrs. Clemens, Mark Twain had taken no notice whatsoever of Christmas. He had never given or received a present and was always terribly annoyed with anyone who even mentioned the day. His secretary, of course, knew this; when she had first heard whispers of my surprise for Mr. Clemens, she had gotten in touch with Mother and told her it would be better if I didn't give Mr. Clemens any gift or talk about Christmas.

Mother had thought the matter over and decided she couldn't spoil my anticipation of the surprise or rob me of any of my joy in Christmas. So she said nothing to me and told Mr. Clemens' secretary that, short of a cataclysm, I couldn't be persuaded not to give my beloved SLC a present. But she did tell me not to talk about my present or Christmas beforehand as it might spoil the "surprise."

Completely unconscious of all this, I scampered down the stairs, while for once Mother lent an unattentive ear to Mr. Clemens as she listened to my approach. At last, a very whirlwind of a figure, I rushed through the door, shouting, "Merry Christmas, Merry Christmas!" I flung my arms around Mr. Clemens' neck, deposited a kiss on his cheek and thrust the package into his hand, crying "Merry Christmas!" again.

As my voice died away, there was a silence during which

Mr. Clemens stood holding the package, looking first at it and then at me, his face revealing nothing of his thoughts. I didn't understand the silence. Things were not going at all as I had expected. Mr. Clemens wasn't excited; he was not responding to my "Merry Christmas," looking at the package, or anything. I was completely puzzled.

"Aren't you going to open your present?" I asked impatiently.

A shadow crossed his face as he came back from the far places into which he had been catapulted by my "Merry Christmas"—a shadow that made his countenance seem like that of someone I didn't know at all. I tightened my arm around his neck and put my face against his. I didn't understand, but I knew something was wrong and instinctively clung to him for comfort.

The shadow lightened; then it disappeared, and his face resumed its natural expression.

"Is this for me"? he asked, almost as though he didn't quite understand and was feeling his way through an unknown country.

The others breathed easier. The dreaded moment had passed. There had been no explosions. But, although the waters were calm, the shore had not yet been reached.

"Of course," I began eagerly. "It's your Christmas present. I've had it for ages. I could hardly wait to give it to you; of course, it isn't actually Christmas yet, but I do think you could open it now while I am still here, don't you?" I'd been brought up on the Christmas-morning package-opening theory, but I did want to be on hand while these especial red ribbons were being untied.

"Certainly it's all right. It's pre-eminently proper that I should open it while you are still here. In fact, if you weren't here, I couldn't open it at all, and then I should perish with curiosity." Mark Twain was smiling now. He sat down in his favorite big chair, and I perched on the arm of it close beside him where I had a good view of the proceedings.

I watched him undo in a few seconds the wrappings I had worked so hard to achieve. At last the knife was exposed to view and was admired by its recipient with all the enthusiasm I had looked for. Each one of the blades and gadgets for smoking which it contained were opened and commented upon. Mr. Clemens announced that he would enjoy his cigars twice as much now that he could cut off their ends with his new knife, which sent me into the clouds with joy that I had really found something he liked.

Just then he turned briskly to his secretary. "What have I got I can give Dorothy for a . . . " he paused, and then added quickly, "a Christmas present?"

The other occupants of the room rejoiced silently. The boat had reached shore with all flags flying. Mark Twain was receiving and *giving* a Christmas present, after all the years that he had ignored the day.

His secretary thought quickly, for nothing must happen to spoil the moment which had turned out so happily.

"How about one of those books that were sent you—the *Joan of Arc?*"

Mr. Clemens exclaimed enthusiastically, "The very thing! Get it and I will write in it."

Then while the book was being procured he told me that it was a special edition of a life of Joan, especially illustrated by a celebrated French artist, M. Louis Maurice Boutet de Monvel; that a few copies of the limited edition had been sent him by the Century Company on account of his own book about Joan. And I quickly understood his present was a rare and unusual one.

It was a long, narrow book bound in lavender, and on the inside of the cover Mr. Clemens wrote, "To Dorothy Quick, with the love of S. L. Clemens, 1907—21 Fifth Avenue."

The actual reading matter was very short, for most of the pages were taken up with the really beautiful illustrations in color. One could almost know the whole of Joan's life without reference to the text, the drawings were so graphic.

Mr. Clemens turned over the pages for me while I sat on the arm of his chair regarding them. The pictures he liked best were one of Joan in her prison talking to her "Saints," and the one of the battle scenes, which was so spirited and realistic that one half expected the knights to continue their charge and to leap out of the pages.

I was very thrilled that I was going to have this book for my own. When Mr. Clemens had finished showing the pictures to me, he put the book in my hands and said, "Merry Christmas, Dorothy dear."

So the spirit of Christmas was brought back into his heart.

While my remembrance of that Christmas has always been a particularly happy one, it has always been tinged a little by sadness, like sunshine viewed through momentary rain. A later Christmas brought tragedy to Mr. Clemens, when his daughter Jean died on Christmas Eve, after trimming the tree for her father and making great plans for the Christmas celebration.

However, that Christmas Day of 1907 was full of gladness, with no hint of sorrow to come.

I took the precious book and then suddenly remembered an old superstition.

"Oh, you've got to give me some silver because I gave you

something sharp!" I said. "And we don't want anything to cut our friendship," I then exclaimed, aghast at the very thought.

Mark Twain put his hand in his pocket and brought out a quarter. "Nothing must ever do that. Nothing could, my superstitious friend." He put the quarter in my hand and closed my fingers firmly over it. "Still, I've always found in life it's better to be on the safe side and not take any chances."

22

The Art of Paying a Compliment

THOUGH THE Joan of Arc book was my first Christmas present from Mr. Clemens, it was by no means the first book—or the last—that he gave me at No. 21. He was always presenting me with books, and I hardly ever returned from a visit to him without one or two volumes in my bag.

In New York, as I have said, I rarely saw Mr. Clemens in the morning. If Miss Clemens wasn't singing and his secretary was busy, I always went to the billiard room and curled up in the window seat to read one of the books I would select from the many shelves. There was a great variety of reading matter, and I was catholic in my tastes and had ambitions to devour them all at some time during my visits. There was nothing I liked better than to read and SLC encouraged me in it for, as he often said, it was my love of reading that had brought us together.

One day Mr. Clemens finished his work earlier than usual and came to the billiard room in search of me. There I was stretched out on the window seat, with a pillow behind my head, Tammany in my lap, and a large, heavy book in my hands. Mr. Clemens, full of curiosity about what I had chosen this time, looked at the title and discovered it was *Ben Hur*.

"That, my dear," he said, "is one of the greatest books that was ever written. But it's too long to read while you are visiting me. You'll get too interested in it and I'll lose your society. So you just put it by for now and take it home with you."

This I did, and I still have the Players Edition of *Ben Hur* with "S. L. Clemens" written on the back of its cover, for he wouldn't hear of my returning it as he said it was the kind of book one should reread as one grew older. "Ten years from now there'll be things in it you don't see at the present time, Dorothy, and ten years after that there'll still be more and again in ten years more. Only, when you've reached my age will you be able to appreciate fully each and every word."

Another time he found me laughing over a red volume entitled *Mark Twain's Library of Humor,* a collection of stories which I thought very amusing. Mr. Clemens told me that that book and its second volume were the only ones of their kind in existence; that it had been gotten together without his knowledge and that as the publishers had used his name without his consent, he had made them destroy the entire edition, with the exception of the two books he had. The plates had also been destroyed so that it could never be reprinted. "Which makes it very unique. So as you like it, I'm going to give it to you and write down all about it in the front of the book." Which he promptly proceeded to do, and this priceless book with its long inscription occupies a place in my library next to his own books, which are even more precious to me.

Mr. Clemens also gave me a fountain pen on one of my visits. He, himself, was never without one and always had his

148

favorite pen of the moment clipped on to his upper vest pocket where it was as much of a fixture as a doctor's thermometer is to him.

Mr. Clemens was very much interested in the development of the fountain pen as the first early version was constantly being improved upon, and when any new ones were brought out they were always sent to him. One Waterman's pen he liked so much that he ordered a lot of them and gave one to everyone of whom he was particularly fond because "It writes so well I will be sure of getting letters in a handwriting I can read." Mr. Paine and I were each presented with one at the same time, and they were presents that were enthusiastically received. I used mine for years until, like the "One Horse Shay," it just dropped apart.

Once I was able to bring a new idea and amusement to Mark Twain—skeleton-signatures. These were made by folding a sheet of paper in half, then straightening it out and writing one's name on the crease, then quickly folding the paper together again and rubbing it on the outside so that the ink would blot. The result was a skeleton-like figure that was invariably amusing. This was immediately tried out with the new pens and rechristened "ghosts" by Mr. Clemens, which was decidedly a better name as they were very wraithlike and ethereal looking.

We made several sets of them. One had "S. L. Clemens" in the center with my ghosts on the sides. Then I made one of my own autograph, which Mr. Clemens immediately embellished. On one side of it he wrote at the appropriate places, "The head, neck, arms, the rest of her," and at the very bottom of the paper, "Dorothy Quick's Ghost—to be looked at from this point."

We had lots of fun with the ghost-signatures for a while,

and everyone that came in had to make one. But after we'd gotten a good collection, the enthusiasm wore off and the ghosts were forgotten.

Mr. Clemens was always interested in fortunetelling and things like that. I don't think it was because he believed in them as much as because he wanted to. At any rate, it was just about the very beginning of the use of handwriting as a science and revealer of character. Mr. Clemens sent specimens of his handwriting anonymously to seven different experts for character analysis, and when six out of the seven reported that "the writer of these lines does not possess a sense of humor," he went into great gales of laughter as though he were bent on immediately disproving their theory. It certainly didn't tend to make him a supporter of the graphology system of character-reading. In fact, he remarked, "So far as I can see it isn't much of a science, but maybe it will improve as it goes along. Most things do or else they get snuffed out entirely. It will be interesting to see what happens to this."

Mark Twain hadn't forgotten his promise to take me to the banquet, but on January 11, when the Lotos Club dinner was held in his honor, I was in bed battling with the bronchitis. My cold wasn't helped at all by the thought of what I was missing, but Mr. Clemens promised that he would make the speech all over again for my benefit at soon as I was well enough to come in. This proved every bit as efficient as the medicine I was taking to aid my recovery, and the Saturday after the dinner I arrived at No. 21 in the best of spirits, full of anticipation of hearing what had gone on.

The first thing Mr. Clemens did was to give me a souvenir of the dinner—the menu. It was a large sheet, rolled like a diploma. In the center was a large three-quarter picture of

Mark Twain in his beloved Oxford gown. I always wore his favorite white when I visited him.

Aug. 12/08.

Dorothy dear, I wrote you a number of days ago, & mailed it to Epping, but I don't think you'll get it, because I couldn't make sure of the address you gave me. If it is Dow, you should write it like this: DOW — not like this: Dow (which is the way you wrote it). Don't ever again write a proper name in any but CAPITALS — do you hear?

But you'll never get this, so why should I go on writing?

With lots of love

SLC

"Innocence at Home" chastises me because of my handwriting, August 12, 1908.

Mr. Clemens in his Oxford robes and cap—a photograph that was particularly lifelike in its portrayal. About it was:

Dinner to
    Samuel L. Clemens, Litt. D.
    by the Lotos Club, New York
    Saturday, January 11, 1908.

Then there was a design of lotos flowers and the old homes of the club and the new one to which it was going. Below Mark Twain's portrait was a woman holding in one hand a scroll on which all of Mr. Clemens' degrees were set forth, and in the other a mask of Mark Twain. All around the margin were small pictures of scenes and characters from his books— very attractive ones.

Mr. Clemens had autographed it for me; just below his picture was his distinctive "Mark Twain," and below that was the menu:

Innocent Oysters Abroad
Roughing it Soup
Huckleberry FinnFish
Joan of Arc filet of beef
Jumping Frog Terrapin
Punch Brothers Punch
Gilded Duck
Hadleyburg Salad
Life on the Mississippi Ice Cream
Prince and Pauper Cake
Pudd'n Head Cheese
White Elephant Coffee

"Goodness!" I exclaimed, as I read the imposing list. "Did you eat all that?"

Mr. Clemens looked wise. "No. I didn't. I stayed through Joan of Arc filet, because I'm fond of Joan and wanted to do her honor, but when it came to the Jumping Frog terrapin, I decided it was time for me to jump! So I said I thought I'd been out of bed pretty late for me and I'd like to take a nap."

My eyes were wide. "And did you?"

He shook his head vigorously. "No, but I got upstairs and stretched out and had a good cigar while they went on eating and talking, and when they got down to the white elephant coffee, I went back greatly refreshed."

"What did you talk about?" I questioned, all eager for the repetition of the speech he had promised.

"Well," he drawled, "President Lawrence got up first and said that they'd given me a dinner fourteen years ago, and seven years ago, and would go on giving me one every seven years. Then Colonel Robert Porter, who went with me to Oxford when I got my degree, was called on to tell the things that had happened then, and he said that he was greatly impressed at the number of people abroad who knew me—the people on the street, even the London policemen—which shows a naïveness on Mr. Porter's part because even I know that London policemen know everything and everybody."

"Why I could have told him everyone knows you—everywhere." I had to put my oar in.

Mr. Clemens laughed heartily. "Next time I must have you along. You know all the good things about me that are right for people to hear. I know the bad ones myself, but of course I'd never tell those."

"What did you say at the dinner?" I wasn't going to be cheated of my speech.

He leaned back in his armchair and then began speaking in his gentle, slow way, with his eyes half-shut as though he were endeavoring to recall, word for word, what he had spoken about.

"Well, I thanked them for their welcome for that night, and seven years back and fourteen years ago, which I'd forgotten to thank them for at the time, and I said I hoped they'd continue the custom of giving me dinners every seven years. I had had it in my mind to join the hosts of another world—I didn't know which—but I'd enjoyed their customs so much I was willing to postpone it for another seven years."

"And then seven more and seven more," I interpolated; not liking the turn the speech had taken, I was too fond of him to laugh as his listeners at the banquet had.

"You little rat, I'll do my best to go on for seven times seven—and, of course, if I had any say about it, I'd be perennial. Don't you want to hear the rest of the speech?"

"Of course I do." I leaned forward eagerly, forgetting my momentary sadness.

"Then I told them how a guest of honor is always in an embarrassing position because compliments have been paid him; that whether you deserved it or not it was hard to talk up to; and then I made them all laugh because I said, 'the other night at the Engineer's Club dinner, when they were all paying Mr. [Andrew] Carnegie discomforting compliments that were not deserved, I tried to help him out with criticisms and references to things nobody understood.' "

He opened his eyes wide and looked at me sagaciously. "Do you know, Dorothy, nobody laughed harder at that than Mr. Carnegie who sat close by?"

We laughed together, and then I urged him to continue with the speech. "What did you say next?"

"Let me see." He got up and began walking back and forth across the room, his hands in his pockets.

"I said, 'They say that you cannot live on bread alone, but I could live on compliments. I do not make any pretence that I dislike compliments. The stronger the better, and I can manage to digest them. I think I have lost so much by not making a collection of compliments, to put them away and take them out again once in a while.' "

"Oh, I wish I'd been there! What came next?" I hadn't taken in the fact that a good deal of the time he was talking with his back to me. I was so used to having him prowl around as he talked that I took it more or less for granted.

Mark Twain went on, "I said I'd written down my compliments to preserve them and I thought they were mighty good and extremely just. Then I read a few."

"Oh, tell them to me." I begged.

"The first was by Hamilton W. Mabie, who said that La Salle was the first one to make a voyage of the Mississippi, but Mark Twain was the first to chart, light, and navigate it for the whole world.

"If that had been published at the time that I issued that book [*Life on the Mississippi*], it would have been money in my pocket. I told them it is a talent by itself to pay compliments gracefully and have them ring true. It's an art by itself."

"I like that compliment. Were there any more?" I asked.

He turned, regarded me with a half-smile on his face. "Oh, yes, indeed. Do you want to hear all of them?"

"I certainly do."

He resumed his walking. "The next was by Albert Bigelow Paine, my biographer. He has been at my elbow for two and one-half years. He says, 'Mark Twain is not merely a great writer, a great philosopher, a great man; he is the supreme expression of the human being, with every human strength— and weakness.'

"Then I told him that my friend W. D. Howells spoke of me as 'first of Hartford, and ultimately of the solar system, not to say of the universe,' and I commented, 'You all know how modest Howells is. If it can be proved that my fame reaches to Neptune and Saturn, that will satisfy even me!'

"Then I mentioned a few stories about Howells and read what Thomas Edison wrote: 'The average American loves his family. If he has any love left over for some other person, he generally selects Mark Twain.' "

"I like that best of all," I said. "Only instead of 'generally' I think he should have said 'always.' " Mr. Clemens had so impressed upon me the importance of words that I was ever on the alert for the right word in the right place.

"I declare, Dorothy, I'll have to write that down to use next time." Mr. Clemens drawled and patted my head as he walked by.

"Weren't there any more compliments?"

"Dozens. But I'm only going to tell you one more. It's a compliment from a little Montana girl which came to me indirectly. She was in a room in which there was a large photograph of me. After gazing at it steadily for a time, she said: 'We've got a John the Baptist like that. Only ours has more trimmings.' I suppose she meant the halo."

That was so funny that I laughed and laughed. After a while, Mr. Clemens joined me and when we finally stopped, he sat down in his big armchair again. I could see a twinkle in his eye and I didn't know what it came from, for it was one of his mischievous twinkles, and I didn't know of any mischief he'd been up to or any joke he could have played.

"Did you tell any more compliments?" I insisted.

"One or two, but if you want to know what they were you'll

just have to read them for yourself. It's too much trouble reading this fine print from a distance."

At this point he handed me the newspaper account of his speech from which he had been quoting his own words.

Now I knew why there had been a mischievous twinkle in his eyes and why he had kept his back turned to me so much. And once more the room resounded to our mirth.

I read the clipping from end to end. He had given me the best of it. There was only one compliment he had left out; it was a gold miner's compliment, given on the occasion of his introduction to an audience in an old log schoolhouse. There were only miners present, and when they wanted someone to introduce Mark Twain's lecture, they selected a miner who didn't want to do it, on the grounds that he had never appeared in public. But he finally consented and this is what he said: "I don't know anything about this man. Anyhow, I only know two things about him. One is, he has never been in jail, and the other is, I don't know why."

He had wound up his speech by a reference to his English trip and explained that he had met the King long years ago and that he regretted that some newspapers had made a point of his talking to the Queen of England with his hat on. "I don't do that with any woman. I did not put it on until she asked me to. Then she *told* me to put it on, and it's a command there. I thought I had carried my American democracy far enough. So I put it on. I have no use for a hat, and never did have.

"Who was it who said that the police of London knew me? Why, the police know me everywhere. There never was a day over there when a policeman did not salute me, and then put up his hand and stop the traffic of the world. They treated me as though I were a duchess."

When I'd finished reading, I looked over at him and said reproachfully. "You didn't tell them a single one of my compliments."

Mr. Clemens put his arm around my shoulder. "I didn't tell them compliments from any of my children. There are some things too near and dear to be shared. Don't ever forget, Dorothy, that the paying of compliments is an art by itself and the receiving of them is an utter joy when they're the real kind."

23

"Continued Letters" from Bermuda

Mr. CLEMENS OFTEN SPOKE TO ME about Andrew Carnegie. Mr. Carnegie was one of his best friends, and Mr. Clemens never refused an invitation to the beautiful Carnegie house if he could help it.

"It's a bit far uptown," he would tell me, "but it makes a very nice drive."

One of the things that impressed me most was Mr. Clemens' account of the tablecloth that Mr. Carnegie greatly prized. It was of the finest white linen and was only used when Mr. Carnegie was entertaining celebrities. They were always asked to write their name on the tablecloth; then it was sent away and embroidered so that it contained the autographs of practically everyone of importance, from royalty down. When Mr. Carnegie went to his castle in Scotland, the tablecloth went along, so that if he entertained anyone of importance for the shooting, their signatures would be added to the already imposing array of names.

"Pretty soon he will have to start a new cloth for this one's getting rather crowded," Mr. Clemens said. "I'm glad to be able to tell you, Dorothy, that my name is in a very conspicuous spot, and where there's no danger of its being covered up by a soup plate."

It was the first time I had ever heard of embroidering a person's handwriting, and I have often wondered if Mr. Carnegie's idea wasn't the forerunner of the vogue for one's own handwriting on lingerie and note paper, which later became so fashionable.

My week ends with Mark Twain kept up regularly throughout the winter, except when I was laid low with the bronchitis or he was similarly afflicted. We had such good times with the theaters, billiards, the Authors' League, and innumerable other things to make the hours fly that it seemed to me I would hardly arrive at No. 21 when it would be time to go home again.

During one of my visits, Mr. Clemens took me to the Museum of Natural History to see the new wing that had just been opened. One of the high officials of the museum took us through and then escorted us behind the scenes, as it were, and showed us how they studied photographs and sketches of the animals for a long time before the sculptors molded the forms over which the real animal skins were stretched. Thus, when they were ready to be placed in the groups that we had just seen up in the hall, the animals looked exactly as they had in real life, with every muscle in its proper place.

I whispered to Mr. Clemens that I thought they were wasting their time studying dead animals and stretching their skins on forms. "They might much better be observing you and what you say and do. That would do the world much more good than seeing how Alaskan bears look in their native habitat, because no one is interested in the bears and everyone is interested in Mark Twain."

And I couldn't for the life of me see why Mr. Clemens and the other gentlemen to whom he repeated the remark were so intensely amused!

Once Mr. Clemens took me to the Hippodrome because he thought it would be good for me to see something youthful.

"You're much too old for your years, Dorothy. I've got to keep you young and I've no objection to taking a 'youth cure' with you!"

I loved the Hippodrome. It was so unusual that even Mr. Clemens was impressed by the girls who marched in and out of the water. He tried to explain the diving-bell system to me, but it was quite beyond my powers of comprehension, especially as he said he was none too sure of it himself.

Greatly to my joy, they had performing elephants, whose achievements were almost unbelievable. As one of them carefully stepped over his trainer who was lying prone on the floor, I noticed Mr. Clemens shake his head somewhat sadly.

"Don't you like it?" I whispered.

"It's a wonderful exhibition of training," Mr. Clemens replied, "but it always makes me feel a little sad to see anything brought down from its high estate—or something meant to be great that doesn't know its own power. That elephant could kill that man with less effort than I could kill a fly. In fact, if thoroughly aroused, it could probably stampede the lot of us and yet because it doesn't know its own power it does tricks when its keeper cracks the whip. And people are like that—ever so many people! They don't know their own possibilities and so they perform just as the elephant does for someone else's bidding, while all the time within them is the driving power of the universe. It's a great pity."

By now, although I didn't quite understand all that he was saying, I was looking very serious myself.

Mr. Clemens saw this and put his hand on mine. "Don't you worry about it, Dorothy. You're too little to help when even grown-ups cannot manage to do anything about it. Anyway, I'm all right. The elephant is intelligent and doesn't know it, but no one can say that about me. I know how intelligent I am and you'll know about you before I get through teaching you."

By now the elephants had finished their act, and Toto the clown was amusing everybody. I joined in the general hilarity, and the lesson in philosophy was over for the day.

In February the good times at No. 21 came to an end temporarily, for right after St. Valentine's Day Mr. Clemens wrote:

> 21 FIFTH AVENUE
> Wednesday an hour after midnight.
>
> I got your Valentine which I prize. Today I got your letter and I thank you for it.
>
> And you didn't take a single prize. You dear little rat, it was a shame and I am sorry.
>
> Clara was very busy or she would have sent you a Valentine. She is grieving now because she forgot it. I've been to a banquet tonight and got away at eleven, which is blessedly early for a banquet. I played billiards for an hour and now I've gone to bed.
>
> I sail for Bermuda on the Bermudan Saturday morning with H. H. Rogers. It is for Mr. Rogers' health. We shall stop at the Princess Hotel in Hamilton. You dear child, I wish you were going. Most lovingly,
>
> SLC

I wished so, too, but it just couldn't be. I had to stay in

Plainfield and go on with my school, even though I hadn't won a prize in the month's history. But I could have letters from him while he was away and could look forward to the time when Mark Twain would be home again.

Mr. Clemens never lost a chance to encourage me in my schoolwork. He was always telling me that each thing I was doing would help me to be an author later, which was the one thing needed to spur me on. In one of his letters he said: "I think it is very nice the faithful industry you are devoting to your studies and the gymnasium, and the drawing lessons. They're a great thing. Drawing will educate your eye and give you a correct perception of forms and proportions which you couldn't get in any other way. I've never had a drawing lesson myself, but I know the great value of that art in training the eye to observe; also to see things as they are. Go on with your pleasant labors."

While, of course, this only made me more anxious than ever to do well with the drawing, I also worked very hard at my other studies. When Mr. Clemens came home I was able to report that I had won a prize—not only for history in both the months he had been away, but for drawing too, which news pleased him very much. He was always so delighted over anything I achieved in my studies that it really did make the labor "pleasant."

The first of March I wrote him that I was in bed with another cold, and he promptly replied:

HAMILTON
BERMUDA, March 10/08

Dorothy dear,

I am so sorry, sorry, *sorry* you are sick. I *know* you ought to come here. This heavenly climate and fine air would soon make

162

you strong and well. It is doing wonders for Mr. Rogers. Can't you come? I don't expect to go home before the 1st or 10th of April. I hope your Mother can bring you. You are a frail little creature, and you need to get away from doctors and let generous and wise nature build you up and make you strong. Come to me, you dear Dorothy! You will be so welcome.

Mr. Rogers is improving so decidedly that he has stopped talking about going back home. So I am hoping and expecting to keep him here until April 11th.

We are having very lively times every day, sailing, driving, walking, lunching, dancing and at night we play billiards, and cards, and never go out to dinners or anywhere else.

I am now so strong that I suppose I could pull up one of these islands by the roots and throw it half way to New York. In fact, I know I could.

Write you? Certainly I shall. I don't intend ever to be too busy to write to my dear Dorothy.

Goodbye, with lots and lots of love.

SLC

The picture he painted was so alluring I did want to go, especially when Mr. Clemens wrote Mother and urged her to bring me, and added Mr. Rogers' invitation to join the party. But there was no use. The doctors, for whom Mr. Clemens had no respect, said I couldn't go to Bermuda and return before really warm weather and there was the all important school to attend as soon as I got well. So there was no choice but for me to write and tell SLC how sorry I was that I couldn't go.

I told him, too, that I noticed he was still prejudiced against dinners and I couldn't understand it as I'd had such a rosy time at the one he'd taken me to. I didn't realize at all how a succession of banquets could become truly monotonous to a man as simple as Mark Twain; for like all truly great people, he had the added attribute of simplicity.

Before he could receive my reply, I had another letter from him, dated two days after the one I had just quoted.

HAMILTON, BERMUDA
March 12/08

My poor little Dorothy,

I hope you are well again and will write a line and tell me so. I wish you were here. You would be on your feet right away.

We are to be here about twenty days yet. We sail for New York April 1st.

It is very pleasant. There is always something going on. Yesterday it was a large garden party at the Governor's and there was music by the best band in the British Army, save one—the Horseguards. I have not heard such lovely music except at the King's Garden Party last Summer when the Horseguards Band played.

Day before yesterday I spent the day on the British cruiser and had a screaming good time. (The screaming was over the yarns in the officers' mess.)

Today five of us men drove to St. George's over beautiful roads with charming scenery and the wonderful blue asters always in sight. Distance twelve miles. And we dined at the hotel. However, on the way there we visited a wonderful cave that was discovered in December by a couple of black boys—the most beautiful cave in the world, I suppose. We descended one hundred and fifty steps and stood in a splendid place two hundred and fifty feet long and thirty or forty wide, with a brilliant lake of clear water under our feet and all the roof overhead splendid with shining stalactites, thousands and thousands brown and pink and other tints, all lighted with acetylene jets.

Every Friday night there's a ball in the hotel and I look on. I go out to teas and lunches but not to dinners. I stay at home

164

nights. There are a lot of lovely sailboats and we often go sailing in them. They are wonderfully handled by colored sailors.

You dear child, if you were only here! There's a little bit of a donkey named Maude and we would make trips to Spanish Point. It is three miles and Maude can go there and the water is crystal clear. But you can't bathe there for lack of bath houses.

Friday, 9 P.M.

This has been a lovely Summer day, very brilliant and not uncomfortably warm. If you would only come you could stop these deadly medicines and soon get well. The Ball has begun and I think I will go down and look on. Dear child, I am taking the liberty of appointing you to membership in my "Aquarium" if you will let me. It consists of five angel fishes and one shad. I am the shad. The device of the club is a very small angel fish pin to be worn on the breast. I will fetch it when I come. I have to wear a flying fish pin until I can get a shad made.

March 16th

The Bermudan has arrived with sixty bags of mail and 250 passengers. She sails tomorrow. We don't sail April 1st. We have postponed to April 11th. I am sorry but Mr. Rogers is improving ever so fast and we want him to stay as long as he will. Bermuda is better than four or five or six million doctors. Don't you forget *that,* dear. With lots of love,

SLC

This is the best example I have of Mark Twain's starting a letter and then putting it by and taking it up again—"continued letters," I called them, and the longer they continued the happier I was.

24

The Aquarium and an Angel Fish Pin

THE AQUARIUM SOUNDED VERY INTRIGUING, and the prospect of being a member of any club that germinated in SLC's brain was so wonderful that I was impatient for his return. I wanted to hear all about it and become a full-fledged member.

I was anxious, too, to receive the badge he spoke of. He had often told me about the beautiful tropical fish with the brilliant coloring that were to be found in the waters of Bermuda, so I knew that the pin would be lovely and was dying to see it.

It seemed a very long time before Mr. Clemens returned, but finally the telephone rang and he announced his arrival at No. 21.

The minute Friday's school was over I rushed home and got ready for the trip into New York. Since I hadn't seen Mr. Clemens for so long a time I was to have extra time with him.

Once I saw SLC, I had to admit the truth of his prognostication, "Bermuda is better than four or five or six million doctors!" for I had never seen him look so well. His cheeks were ruddy and he fairly exuded good health.

"No more bronchitis for me!" he boasted. "Oh, if you could have been along, you'd never have had it—nor to take 77 again."

By "77" he meant Humphrey's No. 77, a special cold tablet put up by the well-known pill people, which eventually would get me over the bronchitis if I took enough of them.

He told me all about Bermuda and quoted his already famous remark for my benefit.

"If an American died and went to Bermuda he would think he's arrived in Heaven."

"Heaven couldn't be more beautiful," he went on. "The long roads winding their way through the most luxuriant foliage beside waters so blue it seems as though the skies have fallen into them. But there's no use my going on talking; you've just got to see it for yourself." Then, paying no attention to his own words, he launched into a further description that would have made anyone who heard it want to leap on the first boat bound for the object of the talk.

He told me all about the Aquarium Club, too, which he said "consists of a few very choice school-girl angel fishes and one slave. I am the slave." Then he pinned the glittering blue-green enamel angelfish on my dress and declared solemnly: "Dorothy Quick, you are now an angel fish—M. A.—which means 'Member of my Aquarium,' and I expect you to do it honor some day."

I was very much impressed with the pin. It was as I had expected it would be, a lovely thing with its brilliant colorings. I wore it proudly and gave SLC a dime immediately because it was sharp.

SLC smiled. "The superstitions sailing at full steam. Well,

I'll take your dime, dear, and keep it for emergencies. Now I've got another present for you and it's not sharp or pointed so you'll be able to save money on it."

I clapped my hands and danced around the billiard table. "It's like Christmas," I said. "I guess I'm glad you went away, it's such fun to have you come back."

He dived into his pockets and brought out a square white box. It didn't take me long to open it. The cotton it contained was soon lifted and there lay the most exquisite bracelet of gold links and enameled lilies! It was such a wonderful present that my enthusiasm ran high and the bracelet ran great danger of being lost or broken in my excitement. Finally it was safely clasped around my wrist by its donor, who remarked as he secured it, "You know, it's more fun giving you things than anything I know. I wish I'd brought along the whole shop."

"If you had I wouldn't have had any words left," I exclaimed.

"Then it's just as well. Besides, I wouldn't want anything to happen to the billiard table and if you got too excited you might knock it over." I knew he was making fun of my antics but I didn't care.

When I said I wouldn't have any words left, I was referring to a kind of game Mark Twain had invented for my benefit. He would give me a word and I would have to make a list of words like it, words that meant the same thing really. For instance, he would say, "Take 'joy,' Dorothy, and see how many other expressions for it you can find."

And I would sit down and rack my brain and write laboriously with a complete disregard for spelling:

JOY
Happiness

Delight
Mirth
Gaiety
Gladness, etc.

Then he'd tell me what words I'd used that were really synonymous and cross out the ones that weren't. "Mirth" I remember he removed because mirth didn't really mean joy. "All this," he said, "is very good practice for you and doesn't do me any harm."

When we were playing pool again I reverted back to the topic of Bermuda. "I do wish I could see a real angel fish."

He marched me over to the mirror and pointed to my reflection. "Have you forgoten you've just become one?"

"Ah, no, I could never forget that. I meant I'd like to see the kind with fins."

Once more SLC laughed heartily. "They say mirth is a great tonic. That's why you're such good medicine for me." Then with one of his lightning changes of humor, he turned serious. "They brought some angel fish up on the boat for the Aquarium. We will go see them tomorrow afternoon."

True to his word, the very next day found us riding down Fifth Avenue. After a while the carriage stopped at Battery Park, in front of the long walk that led to the aquarium.

"Why," I exclaimed, "It looks more like a fort than a fish bowl!"

"That shows good power of observation on your part, Dorothy." SLC helped me down out of the carriage as he spoke. "It once was a fort. Over a hundred years ago it was built to defend New York and called the South West Island. This was an island then, and was quite a little ways from the mainland with a bridge to connect it."

By now we were walking up a very solid path, hand in hand. "Where did the water go? There isn't any now," I remarked, even though it was perfectly obvious.

"The water was drained out and filled in with earth until it was made as it is now. Troops used to march here when the Park was the City's parade ground."

"You know everything." I was properly awed by his wisdom.

"I believe I do at that," he admitted modestly. Then, chuckling a little, he said, "There are one or two things, though, I'm not quite sure about even now."

I could see the telltale twinkle in his eye. "What?" I asked.

"That's the kind of a secret I never give away. You're the only person who knows even that much. See that you keep it dark!" he whispered, like a real conspirator. "I *will* tell you about the aquarium, though, for that is good for you to know. From a fort the name was changed to 'Castle Clinton' and it was embellished until it actually looked like a castle. Then the Federal Government gave it to the City and it was turned into 'Castle Garden' and its real life began. Ever so many things happened during that phase of its existence, both interesting and historical. Lafayette was entertained here in 1824; and Jenny Lind, the most famous singer of her day, gave her first concert in America behind these very walls."

He pointed to the aquarium. By now we had drawn quite close to it so there wasn't much more time for information, but he did tell me that after the Castle Garden epoch of its history, it was an immigration bureau and that in 1896 it was made the aquarium, adding, "Where you're going to see an angel fish, Dorothy."

But fate was against the fulfillment of his prophecy. When we went inside, Mr. Clemens was greeted by one of the officials, who said he would escort us through. When Mr. Clemens asked to see the angelfish first, we were told the sad news that the angelfish had died. "No matter what we do, we can't keep them in this climate. They only thrive in their native habitat," the official announced regretfully.

His regret was not half as poignant as ours. To me it was a very real and bitter disappointment. Mr. Clemens sighed a little before he said, "Well, you'll just have to come to Bermuda to see the most brilliant and lovely fish the ocean has. But as long as we're here, we'll just have a look around." So we were escorted all over the aquarium.

I loved the quiet coolness of the place and found the big glass tanks in which the fish were swimming quite fascinating. I didn't like the eel-like variety of fish and shuddered away from the octopus, while even Mr. Clemens admitted he was glad the glass was strong.

I said it was a pity that the octopus couldn't have died instead of the angelfish. SLC gave another glance at the horrible creature and remarked, "It looks as thought it could survive anything—even a German dinner."

We spent at least two hours being shown about. Here, just as at the Museum of Natural History, we were shown all the things the ordinary visitor would never see. Mark Twain's name proved an "Open sesame!" to every door that had "No Admittance" on it, so that we not only saw a great many fish that were not yet on exhibition, but we also got a very good idea of the inside workings of the aquarium and how it was run. Mr. Clemens finally declared he was "just about ready to take over the job myself."

On the way home I told him I hadn't had such a good time since he went away, and SLC said, "That's good to hear," and was as pleased over the success of the day's outing as I.

25

Our Last Times at No. 21 Fifth Avenue

THE NEXT WEEK END that I had planned to spend with Mr. Clemens, I had a cold and was forced to put my visit off until the following Saturday.

On Sunday I was able to write to SLC that my cold was better and I didn't have pinkeye as the doctors had thought, to which letter he replied:

> 21 FIFTH AVENUE
> Tuesday evening
>
> *You dear Little Dorothy,*
> It is very fortunate that you escaped the pink eye, for although a cold is bad, pink eye is worse, and is a stubborn and painful malady.
> I shall look for you Saturday morning with high anticipation. We've got a box for "Girls"—and they say it is very good and is clean and wholesome and hasn't any of that horrible ballet dancing in it such as we saw last Saturday. Margaret Illington has been trying to get into our Aquarium and I wouldn't let her, but

Sunday night she came here to dinner with her husband, Daniel Frohman, and she was dressed for twelve years and had pink ribbons at the back of her neck and looked about fourteen years old and so I admitted her as an angel fish and pinned a badge on her bosom. There are lots of lady candidates but I guess we won't let any more in—unless perhaps Billie Burke.

I've got something for you. It cost ten cents.

I haven't seen the kittens lately, but Tammany came up Sunday night and jumped upon the table and helped me play billiards uninvited.

With lots and lots of love, SLC

We must start the Authors' league again.

SLC

It always seemed to me that whenever I was ill something particularly entrancing happened at No. 21. I hated missing the matinee even though the ballet dancing had been "horrible," and to think that I could have seen Margaret Illington "dressed for twelve years old" was even harder to smile away. I made up my mind that I certainly was going to be all right and able to go see "Girls"—and I was.

To this day I remember the leading lady's putting black shoe polish on her heel so the hole in her black stocking wouldn't show. This happened in the very first act, and there was no more attentive listener in the audience than one Dorothy Quick, who sat drawn up to her full height, literally stiff with attention, beside Mr. Clemens in the box he had taken.

It was during this visit that I first heard of the new house that was even then in the process of being built for Mark Twain at Redding, Connecticut. SLC mentioned it very casually on Saturday evening while we were playing billiards.

"Once I get up country I don't suppose you'll be able to come so often for week-ends."

I was all curiosity to know what "up country" meant; and he proceeded to explain about the new house and told me he had decided the city was too hectic for him, that he needed the good, fresh country air, and that he thought we could have even better times at Redding than we had at No. 21.

Quite suddenly I felt very sad. It would be the end of something that had been very precious. I had grown to love the friendly old mansion that had taken me to its heart and given me so many wonderful times. Hastily, I tried to express a little of what was passing through my mind.

SLC was sad, too, for just as he had said, he realized I couldn't come as often to Connecticut as I had to New York. But he stoutly maintained that we'd have just as much fun and that if I couldn't make the trip for overnight, I'd have to spend my vacations and come for long visits in the summer, which prospect cheered us both up.

By now the affection between us was a really vital thing, and the contemplation of a long separation was very depressing.

SLC went on to tell me all about the charms of Redding and how Mr. Paine had a house near by. He enlarged on the beautiful scenery and the fun we would have, until he had literally talked us out of the depression and we were playing billiards merrily again.

During this visit the Authors' League, which had been entirely neglected during SCL's absence, was started again, as he said it should be in his letter. Once more the stories were written, criticised, and rewritten.

During my stay I wrote one story with which he was quite pleased—so much so that after I had returned home with it he wrote and asked me to send it back to him. This I did, but not before I had made a few changes that I thought still further improved it. This apparently was not what Mr. Clemens wanted, for he promptly wrote:

> 21 FIFTH AVENUE
> Tuesday Evening
> April 28/08

Oh, you dear Dorothy,
You have changed the story! You little rascal! You have put things in it that were not there before and I want it *just as it was.* Be a good child and send me the original Mss., I will be sure and send it back to you.

Of course you did very well in the play. I knew you would.

Dear heart, can't you come up Saturday after next and play billiards and go to a matinee and stay over until Monday? Can't you? Won't you? I hope so. Ask your Mother if you may come.

I shan't be here long, only a month, then our new house in the country will be finished. And you must come there as soon as you can. There will be a bed in your room for your Mother.

I haven't seen a cat since you went away, until tonight. Then Tammany came up to play billiards.

> SLC

I like the story in its changed form, but I think I like the former form a little the best.

Needless to say, I sent the original version of the story to him at once. When a little later I followed it, SLC pointed out to me where my changes had been good and where they had fallen down, and he said, "I'll just keep this, if you don't mind."

I didn't mind anything he did, but when we had finished working on it, I asked, "Whatever do you want to keep the story for?"

SLC looked very wise as he glanced at me from underneath

his heavy eyebrows. "You just keep on reading my books, Dorothy dear—and some day you'll find out."

And though I spent a great deal of time and energy coaxing for further information, I couldn't get him to say any more.

The play which he mentioned in his letter had been one in which I was appearing in the parish house of the Grace Episcopal Church. The cast was composed of members of the Sunday-school class to which I belonged. Mr. Clemens had been especially interested in my dramatic debut, for it was to be in a one-act play by his friend, W. D. Howells. He had gone over it once or twice with me to be sure I got the proper inflection in my speeches. I was enacting an Irish maid, and he said he knew a lot about the Irish. He saw that my brogue was perfect, but we were so busy enjoying ourselves that I hadn't time to properly memorize the lines.

I wasn't worried about them as I had a very quick memory, and long ago I had decided that by keeping the script at the entrance and going over one very long speech just before I went "on," I would be able to manage without being at rehearsals. The rehearsals interfered with my visits to No. 21, and I didn't want to miss a second with my friend. I had promised to be all ready for the part even though I didn't rehearse with the rest of the cast.

This had seemed a very good arrangement, and everyone understood my wanting to be with Mark Twain. But when I went to the dress rehearsal on my return from No. 21, I discovered, to my horror, that I was on the stage from the beginning of the play until a good while after the long speech! Neither Mr. Clemens nor I had noticed that the stage directions called for the maid's presence on the stage all the time.

I spent my entire time between the dress rehearsal and the actual performance that night learning the speech. Mr. Clemens was very amused later when I told him about it, and was deeply regretful that he had been unable to come out for the play as he had wanted to. "Only business could have kept me away," he assured me. "But it's a good lesson that one should always be ready for any emergency."

Whenever I thought that the good times at No. 21 would soon be ended, I felt as though a sponge had been wiped over my slate of joy—not enough to eradicate any of the figures that stood for so much happiness, but just enough to blurr them a little. I did love No. 21. I revelled in its old-fashioned charm, and whenever I went up the stone steps, my heart would beat faster in anticipation of the pleasures waiting within.

Privately I didn't think any house "up country" could be nearly so attractive. It takes houses time to acquire charm from their owners. No. 21 was steeped in the personality of Mark Twain. The new house couldn't have the same atmosphere to begin with. I was quite sure of that. Nevertheless, I couldn't help being gradually drawn into taking an interest in it.

In the mornings, while Mr. Clemens was busy, I would sometimes be allowed to help choose fittings for the country place. After a doorknob had been selected to use on the long French windows because I liked it best of the number that had been brought in, I felt that I had actually had a part in the construction of the house. In fact, I did more than Mr. Clemens himself, for he steadily refused to have anything to do with the details, large or small, and left the whole thing in the capable hands of the architect to whom he had entrusted it, John Mead Howells, who was the son of his old friend William Dean Howells, and already well known in his own right as an architect. So Mr. Clemens had no fears for the ultimate result, and

177

beyond saying, "I want lots of sunshine, a billiard room and an orchestrelle," he refused to be consulted about anything that was going on.

"I just want to walk in when it is finished," was his pronouncement, and he stuck to it. He would not even look at the plans or help in any way with the construction or furnishing.

I wished I could emulate his lack of curiosity, but I couldn't. I had a very inquiring nature, so I looked at the blueprints, and was quite sure that whatever else the new house would be when it was finished, it would, at least, be a worthy setting for its master.

As is the way with all new projects, it was not ready as soon as had been anticipated, so I had many more happy week ends with Mark Twain at No. 21.

In a letter written on Tuesday, May 8, 1908, SLC wrote underneath the date, "Joan of Arc's Day," which was just one more illustration of how fond he was of the Maid and how much she was in his thoughts. He also said:

I hope you are well over your bronchitis by this time and that you will be careful and not bring on another attack for I know a great deal about that disease by experience and if one wants to be sick and must be sick, it's best to try something else.

Mr. Clemens didn't have much use for bronchitis nor had I at that point, for I was missing another visit. But I made up for it by spending the first Saturday in June with him, which was, although I didn't know it at the time, my last stay at No. 21 Fifth Avenue. If I had known it, I should have prolonged each minute and spent all night playing billiards, which would have pleased Mr. Clemens tremendously, for he liked nothing better than playing on into the small hours of the morning.

But luckily I did not know it was the last time I would climb those stone steps to hear Mr. Clemens' hearty "Hello, Dorothy!" when the front door was opened. If I had, when I left I should have probably been dissolved in tears, for I hated "last times" and saying good-by to anything that I loved so much.

Not knowing, I left in the best of spirits, for I was to come back the next week end, and in the meantime Mr. Clemens was going to come out to my school's commencement in June. I was all aflutter with excitement over the thought, to say nothing of my schoolmates.

But we were doomed to disappointment. Mr. Clemens couldn't come, as he was called to Boston the day before on some very important business engagement which could not be postponed. He called me up to break the bad news and consoled me by telling of the wonderful plans he had made for the week end.

But that, too, didn't work out. I did too much at the commencement festivities, and I had to telephone him and say I couldn't come in. At the same time I told him that I had farmed out my pets for the summer among my friends who were not going away.

On that Sunday he wrote me the last letter I was to receive from him with the familiar "21 Fifth Avenue" engraved in black on the small ivory-tinted note paper he always used:

21 Fifth Avenue
Sunday, June 14/08

I am so sorry, dear heart, that I could not come to commencement for I would have been glad to see your school and meet your friends.

My secretary is working very hard these days getting the new house up country ready. Of course it requires a world of labor to get a new house in shape. She has been at it day and night and past week and has gotten all the furniture and the orchestrelle and a billiard table in at last and says the house will be ready for me next Thursday. I shan't be able to leave here until next Thursday afternoon, then I'll go. I am sure I will like the house from all accounts. I think you will like it too when you come to pay me a visit.

You careless child! How do you know you can trust Claire and Dorothea and Nellie? As for me, I never expect to see those rabbits nor that bird nor that goldfish again. I wish now that I had gone to Plainfield while they were still alive.

I wish you wouldn't be sick so much, dear. You seem to be always travelling from one malady to another and it grieves me. Get well and stay well, won't you?

SLC

26

"Innocence at Home" in Redding

ABOUT THIS TIME Mark Twain was asked if there wasn't anything special he would like to have in the new house that was so nearly finished—anything he would particularly desire. He thought a minute and then said, "I am quite sure everything will be as I want it. I'd only like to see Dorothy Quick's face when I open the front door."

Mother was immediately gotten in touch with, and she said that I was much better and she was sure I would be all right by Thursday. So a surprise was planned for Mr. Clemens. Since he wouldn't arrive at Redding until the afternoon, Mother was to take me up in the morning. Nothing would be said about me, but when SLC came he would be taken at once to the billiard room and find me sitting on the table! It was a beautiful idea, but bronchitis is no respecter of plans. Just when everything was looking rosy for the success of the surprise, the return attack SLC had warned me against laid heavy hands upon me and back to bed I went.

So instead of popping up from the billiard table with the "Welcome Home!" I had been carefully rehearsing, I could only send a telegram. But although I wasn't there to fling my arms about his neck and give him the personal welcome that I had been looking forward to, my every thought was with him that day when he saw his new home for the first time. As someone has said, our thoughts are ourselves, so I felt that at least I was represented at the home-coming.

Finally I was taken to Atlantic City to get rid of my cold, and while there I received a letter from SLC who had now heard of the surprise that hadn't come off, and was as regretful as I was about it. This letter was written on the same ivory-tinted paper he liked, but instead of the black "21 Fifth Avenue" was:

INNOCENCE AT HOME
REDDING
CONNECTICUT

And it was done in bright red, which I liked ever so much better, it was so gay.

He said that I was having too good a time because he wasn't in it, that nevertheless he was glad and wouldn't break into it now, but that he would have to before long for I must come and pay him a visit. About the new house he wrote:

"Innocence at Home" is the right name for this house because it describes me and describes the Aquarium Club. What do you think?

The billiard room downstairs is the Aquarium's Headquarters. There framed photographs are being hung around its walls.

The architect built and furnished the house without any help or advice from me and the result is entirely to my satisfaction. It is charmingly quiet with nothing in sight but woodsy hills and rolling country.

We brought Tammany along."

I was certainly glad to hear that the cat to whom I had grown very attached would be at Redding. I did my very best to get well quickly so I could make the promised visit. Soon I was all over the cold, and a definite date was set for my coming to Redding. Mr. Clemens was in Boston with Mr. Paine, so it was arranged that we would meet them at the South Norwalk Station on their way back from Boston and all go to Redding together.

Several letters flew back and forth, as Mr. Clemens was very meticulous in such matters and didn't want any hitch to occur in his plans. Mr. Paine wrote the exact train to take. So, armed with all the necessary information, Mother and I started off.

Our train got in a few minutes after the one Mr. Clemens and Mr. Paine had come on, and they were waiting for us on the platform when we arrived. It was a very happy reunion. I was so glad to see SLC again.

After the first enthusiastic greetings were over, we were hustled off to a waiting automobile by Mr. Clemens, who didn't want to lose any time showing off his new possessions.

We had a lovely drive over the beautiful rolling Connecticut country. But when we exclaimed over the vistas, SLC said that so far as views were concerned, he had the pick of the entire state, and that we'd better save our "ohs" and "ahs" until we stood in his loggia and saw what he could do for us.

As usual, when I was with Mr. Clemens, it was a bright, sunshiny day, so my first vision of "Innocence at Home" showed a long, low, Italian-villa-type of house etched against a bright blue sky, in which white clouds that looked as though they were blossoms swept from gigantic apple trees floated

183

lazily. Sunshine poured down upon the house until it seemed as though a heavenly spotlight had been turned on it for our benefit. It stood out from the background of dark trees and hills like a picture painted by a master hand.

It resembled a beautiful stage-setting. The white stucco house with its red roof fitted into the landscape so perfectly that it was difficult to believe it had not always been a part of it. The doors and windows on the lower floor were all arched, and Mr. Clemens pointed with pride to the arches of the loggia at one end.

We saw all this from the distance as we drove up the hill. When we reached the doorway, there was Claude waiting to welcome us. SLC hurried me into the house with no loss of time. He was so very eager to point out all its beauties.

We stepped at once into a large hall which opened onto the dining room which, in its turn, led to a brick terrace that ran the whole length of the house in the rear. From the terrace one looked down graded lawns that sloped through a lovely garden toward a Greek pergola. A path went from the brick steps of the terrace to the pergola, which had as its background the green of the Connecticut hills, and the dark colors made the white marble seem all the more snowy.

"Now what do you think of my view?" SLC asked proudly, and added, "I don't care how many ohs and ahs you use."

Our response was quite satisfactory, for he literally beamed with pleasure over the "ohs" and "ahs" I expressed as I danced around him—too excited to keep still.

I would have liked to linger much longer beside the open French windows which commanded such an outlook, but Mr. Clemens wanted me to see everything.

Next he took us across the hall to a small room which was

a sort of den, library, and writing room and then allowed the full glory of the living room to break upon us.

It was a large room of magnificent proportions, for it ran almost the length of the house and went from front to back. The orchestrelle was in the center of the wall on the pergola side, the back of the house. The whole room was built around it and splendidly furnished with the most comfortable of chairs and couches. There were plenty of tables, lavishly appointed with the smoking accessories that were so necessary to Mark Twain's comfort. The room was the epitome of all anyone could ask for, not only for comfort but for charm. Directly opposite the door which we had entered was the doorway to the loggia.

"This is where I expect to spend my old age," SLC announced.

The loggia was the most attractive of its kind I had ever seen. It was composed of a series of arches supported by pillars that merged into a domed ceiling. It was open on three sides and had a wonderful sweep of air and sunshine. The furniture was wicker, which looked as though it had been made solely with the idea of comfortable relaxation for its occupant in mind. The floor was brick, and one could step out from under the arches to the terrace in the rear.

Without giving me enough time to take it all in, SLC swept me back through the living room, across the hall, into the billiard room which was on the front of the house and as long as the living room, though not so wide.

"Here is the official headquarters of the Aquarium, just as I told you it would be!" Mr. Clemens announced and then pointed. "See the angel fishes? And look, there is the Indian Princess one of you we took in Tuxedo!"

And there on the red wall hung the photograph right in

the center. There were pictures of other Angel Fish that I was very curious to see, for I had never met any of the other members of the club, except Miss Illington. There, framed, were pictures of real angelfish too, hung in between the photographs, and SLC told me that he wanted each M. A. (Member of the Aquarium) to choose an actual representative of one of the brilliant fish to stand for that member, and to autograph the fish selected so that it would be entirely her own. But he didn't let me make my choice then for I had to see the culinary department and greet Katy and the other servants that I remembered from No. 21, and see the upstairs.

Later on I did go over the fish pictures carefully and chose a gorgeous specimen to represent me—a water color of an angelfish, with lovely colorings of turquoise blue that shaded into deep ultramarine. I signed my name on it with much pride. That, however, was the next day.

After looking over the kitchen, which was very new and modern in every way, Mr. Clemens took me upstairs. To the left was Mr. Clemens' room, with his great big mahogany bed from No. 21, of which he was so fond. At the extreme end Miss Clara Clemens had a suite of rooms that hadn't been furnished as yet. She was in Europe fulfilling concert engagements and wouldn't return until fall, so there was no hurry about getting them done, and "She might have some ideas of her own about it," Mr. Clemens remarked.

Over the dining room was an upstairs library, and to the right was a guest room into which Mother and I were ushered and told that it was "my" room for as long as I could occupy it.

The whole house was beautifully done and in exquisite taste. Furthermore, it didn't have that "new" look I had dreaded. Already it reflected its owner's personality. I didn't wonder that Mr. Clemens was "entirely satisfied with the result."

186

27

Mark Twain, the Actor

BEFORE I HAD COME TO Redding, Mark Twain had written me:

Dorothy dear,
Bring with you a doll about eight inches long. Paine's little daughter, Frances, will fetch a doll when she comes up the hill to visit you and you and she will have a fine domestic time together.
With lots of love,

SLC

Frances is a doll enthusiast.

Mr. Clemens didn't want me to suffer any loss of caste by not having the ability to produce a doll when Miss Paine came to call. It was especially sweet and thoughtful of him, for never once in all the times I had been with him had dolls come into the picture. We'd been too busy doing other things, but he wasn't going to have me left out of anything.

I was too interested in books and writing to play very much

with dolls, but I had a large collection, of which I was very proud. My grandparents had brought me dolls from all parts of the world, and as they were globe-trotters, I had dolls in native costumes from innumerable countries. I also had several of the domestic variety, so that it was difficult to choose which one to take with me. Finally I selected a baby doll from the "family"; she had large blue eyes and, what was even better, a trunkful of clothes. So I brought her along, trunk and all, which proved very satisfactory, for when Frances Paine came up the hill to play with her "child," the dolls were introduced and got along as well as their owners.

Frances was a very sweet, appealing child and we struck up such a companionship that Frances was asked to come up to the big house and stay part of the time that I was there.

Life at Redding was very much a repetition of the days at Tuxedo, except that here Mr. Clemens *never* appeared in the mornings. He would keep to his room until just before luncheon, when he would come down to find us in the loggia.

One of my most vivid recollections of him at Redding is of one day when he came down about twelve-thirty, a Turkish towel around his shoulders, his hair all damp and clinging to his head as I had never seen it before.

"I've just washed my hair," he surprised me by saying, "and now I've come down to let the sun dry it for me." He put a chaise longue where it would be entirely out of the shade and relaxed into it. Gradually, as it dried, his hair stood out more and more from his face until at last it was a cloud of white aureoled by sunshine, and as soft as any swansdown powder puff.

At luncheon he would always entertain us with the funniest of stories, or else read from his own books. Afterward we would all sit out on the loggia, while from inside would come the soft strains of the orchestrelle. The music, as it filtered through the open doors and windows, lent a touch of enchantment to the scene which made it almost unreal in its beauty.

This was what Mr. Clemens enjoyed most in Redding—the long hours in the sun, the music, and the games.

Billiards, of course, was not neglected. There wasn't a morning, afternoon, or evening when the balls weren't "knocked about" for a good part of the time.

SLC and I always played, and sometimes Mother joined in, as did Mr. Paine, who came up at least once every twenty-four hours from his own house which was down the hill just a little way.

But it was "Hearts" that took first place at Redding. Mr. Clemens didn't seem to have quite so much energy as he had before, and was very content to sit at the card table and play the game of which by now he had become a very ardent partisan. Hearts would go on for hours and we all played. Frances was even willing to desert her dolls for the amusement. Anyone else who happened to be there was always pressed into the game by SLC, so that it was lucky that it was an elastic game.

Mr. Clemens was never so happy as when he had a number of congenial people around him, and he ruled his little household with a kindly despotism and accepted the homage he always inspired in his own gracious and lovable way.

He had great fun at Hearts, passing on the black queen, and always managing to get rid of her. He always contrived to win, too, although generally I ran him rather close for first place. But just when I was really getting ahead, he would see that the queen would fall on one of my tricks, which meant the end of my prospects for winning. As he did so, SLC would look in my direction and pull one eyebrow up a great deal higher than the other and drawl very innocently, "I was so sorry that I had to do that, dear heart. It just happened to be unavoidable." And he and I would both smile, just as though we didn't know he had done it on purpose.

Whenever he gave anyone the queen or a heart that counted against the recipient, he would do it in a very naïve manner and pretend to be surprised. So amusingly was this done that no one could mind losing. In fact, it added 50 per cent to the fun of the game.

Hearts would keep up until tea time. When Claude appeared with the tea tray, it was the signal to stop. Generally we had tea in the loggia, but sometimes Claude would serve it out under the trees of which Mr. Clemens was so proud. He would then look around and say that it was quite as much fun as having tea at Buckingham Palace. And I really believe he meant it, for he had a great capacity for enjoyment and his own pleasure was always heightened by sharing someone else's. Remembering his account of the royal garden party which he had attended in London not very long before, I wondered if anything could be quite so nice.

I had been very impressed by his account of the beautiful palace grounds with their velvety green lawns, flower-bordered walks, and age-old trees; the majestic palace looking down at the assembled throngs; the royal tent under which their Majesties, King Edward VII and Queen Alexandria had received him; the other tent for lesser dignitaries; and lastly the long tent with the silver gilt-laden tables that were "literally sinking in the middle with the weight of the delicacies piled upon them."

I recalled how he had described the crowds of people in which Indian princes with their gleaming jewels and resplendent robes had rubbed elbows with simple English misses in frilly organdy. "And over it all, Dorothy," he had said, "was

190

the heavenly music of the Guard's Band—the most stirring music I have ever heard. For once I almost forgot to talk. You'll notice I said 'almost.' I'd have to be pretty far gone when I couldn't find something to say."

All that! And yet he forgot the glamour and the beauty of it in the fun he was having over Frances' and my dolls' tea parties.

There never was a time when I stayed with Mark Twain that he didn't have something brand new by way of amusement for me.

At Redding it was charades. I discovered that Mr. Clemens loved to act, and at the same time he found out that I did, too, so each day he planned a word to act. It was great fun for we dressed up for the parts, and he always arranged some kind of scenic background, even though it might only be a screen.

SLC, Frances, and I were the performers, and the other members of the household had to guess the word which had been so well schemed by Mr. Clemens that a great deal of the time the actors came off victorious. "And no one can say we didn't act it out eloquently, either," Mr. Clemens would say when the onlookers gave up, and no one contradicted him.

Sometimes we called upon the audience to furnish appropriate music on the orchestrelle, and once in a great while they were consulted about costume details.

The word I liked best of all was "mosquito." For the first syllable SLC wound a marvelous yellow scarf turban-fashion around his head and draped a large piece of Indian embroidery over his shoulders. Then with a prayer rug under his arm he walked across the end of the living room, which was the stage.

Suddenly he pretended to hear the call to prayer. He threw his two arms upward to where the supposed caller of the faithful was. Then, just as any true worshipper of the East, he spread his prayer rug on the floor and knelt in the direction of Mecca and said his prayers to Allah. When he had finished his pantomime, he rolled up his rug and after a final bow at the spot where the Mosque should have been, he shuffled slowly out of the room, having portrayed the word "mosque" in a very realistic manner.

I had my chance at histrionics in the next syllable, "key." Mr. Clemens still kept his turban but added an Oriental dressing gown and a blue worsted beard to his props. I was truly a fetching figure with trailing chiffon veils of crimson, borrowed for the occasion. Together we acted out a five-minute version of the old fairy story in pantomime. Mr. Clemens was Bluebeard and said good-by to me very touchingly, at the last minute giving me a bunch of keys with a very obvious caution that one of them must not be used. Then he stalked off, and I was left alone with the keys in hand, a prey to a truly feminine curiosity. I walked up and down in front of the screen that represented the door behind which I must not look. I peered in through the imaginary keyhole. I tried to be firm-minded, just as Bluebeard's wife had been; but at last, overcome by the longing to know what was inside, I inserted the key, moving the screen a little so I could see the fatal chamber.

By this time I had worked myself up to such a pitch that I could almost see the gory bodies of Bluebeard's other wives hanging there. I gave one glance and then emitted a blood-curdling scream and fell fainting to the floor on a large cushion Mr. Clemens had conveniently placed beforehand.

A wave of applause greeted me. Looking up, all I could see was SLC waving his blue beard at me and shouting, "I couldn't have done it better myself," at which compliment the fainting lady recovered sufficiently to take a bow and rejoin her fellow Thespians.

The next and last syllable was Frances'. As the "toe," she had the stage all to herself, and she walked across it and stubbed her toe most artistically for the benefit of her "public."

The whole word was done by the entire company. We sat and drank very real and delicious tea furnished by Claude and remembered our parts long enough to occasionally hit an imaginary mosquito on our ankles.

The audience guessed the word, but they all agreed it was one of the most effective we had done.

Sometimes we would do them in the evening when we had watched the sunset and had after-dinner coffee out on the terrace. The actors and audience would go down to the pergola. The audience would take their seats on the marble benches, and the actors would act out their word in the dim twilight. Sometimes the moon would come up, and the white marble columns of the summerhouse with the moonlight streaming through them made a setting indescribably lovely.

One of the words we did in the pergola was "dogmatic." SLC divided it up into "dog-mat-ic." Frances did the first, walking through the pergola calling "Prince" to follow her. For the next syllable I vigorously swept an invisible mat. Mr. Clemens did the last syllable himself by portraying a slightly inebriated gentleman. His "ic's" were most realistic. His white-clad figure, reeling in and out of the columns in a perfect presentation of his assumed character, was a sight I shall never forget. The moon had turned his hair to pure silver and cast an unearthly glamour over the very earthy man he was acting.

The whole word was done by SLC and myself. He was supposed to be a man with a very strong temper laying down the law to his wife—dogmatic.

The representation of the last syllable by Mr. Clemens was such a success and brought forth so must applause from the spectators that SLC often chose words ending in "-sic" so he could delight the audience again and again with his fascinating conception of a man who had had a "bit too much."

Once he brought tears to everyone's eyes by doing "gravity." Taking "grave" for the first syllable, he took a spade and pretended to dig a grave in such a realistic manner that he had his entire audience in tears before he had finished. And no one could guess the word afterward, for they had been so much affected by his art that they had quite forgotten to think of the game they were playing.

One thing the charades at Redding proved. The stage lost a great artist when Mark Twain turned to letters.

28

Burglaries,
and Redding Mourns Tammany

MARK TWAIN TOOK AN ACTIVE PART in the affairs of the little
Connecticut town of which he had become a resident. One
day at luncheon he announced that we were all to go to the
dedication of the new public library and that he thought it
would be nice if some kind of costumes could be "rigged" up
for Frances and me.

After a great deal of deliberation it was decided that the most
authentic costumes that we could wear on such short notice
would be Japanese, for we had plenty of Japanese kimonos.
So we were arrayed in splendor, with huge chrysanthemums
on either side of our faces. We also had little paper parasols
which Mr. Clemens said we "twirled very fetchingly."

He had several words that he used a great deal with all their
various ramifications. One of these was "fetch," another, "brilliant," and he was very fond of the expression "You little rat."
Personally I disliked the idea of a rat extremely, and if anyone had told me I could enjoy being called one before I met

Mr. Clemens, I would promptly have made faces of disbelief. But then I had never heard Mark Twain say, "Oh, you little rat, you've done it again!" on the rare occasions when a managed to slip the black queen to him when we were playing Hearts, or "You dear little rat, I'm going to miss you when you're gone!" Sometimes it is the way you say things that counts more than the actual words; and whenever SLC used "You little rat," I knew it meant just the same as when he called me "Dear heart," and I grew to love it.

At the library's dedication SLC made a short speech, and after the ceremonies were over he stayed and made everyone happy by talking to them. Mr. Paine took pictures of the two Japanese girls as they ran across the lawn. I had had my camera out all ready to put in the bags when we were packing for the visit and then very stupidly had forgotten it, so there were no pictures taken to illustrate the days at Redding as there had been at Tuxedo.

There was not an Authors' League in progress either. Somehow the country air seemed to produce laziness so far as work was concerned, a sort of living each day for the enjoyment it contained. We were too busy playing to start work, and there were always too many people around.

"It doesn't hurt anyone to relax completely and give their brains a rest," Mr. Clemens said in reference to his own work. "I'm taking a holiday so I guess you'd better track along."

Still he hadn't let me forget that I was someday to be an author, for he would take me for long walks through the woods which surrounded the house, and as we walked along he would speak of the art of writing and story-construction.

"Always remember, Dorothy, to catch the attention of your reader in the opening paragraph. Once you've caught your fish, you're sure to land him unless you do something foolish

later on and let him get away," was one of the things he used
to say.

"The beginning and end of a story are the most important.
If you must let down—although, mind, I don't advise it—the
middle's the best place. It's the first and the last bite of cake
that makes the most impression."

"Don't have too much description at a time. Vary it with
conversation. There's nothing so tiresome as page after page of
solid print. Short paragraphs are often a lure to the reader's
eye."

"Know what you want to say before you begin and then
stick to it. Don't let your characters run away with your story.
Remember, every bit of writing that lives continues to exist
because it has captured in some way the spirit of the author
of its being."

All these maxims and many more were poured into my re-
ceptive ears. I was like a sponge absorbing water. My friend's
wisdom was being caught up by my brain and stored away
for further use almost without my realizing it.

During these walks SLC forgot that I was a child and talked
to me as one writer might talk to another. To me our strolls
through the woods were the outstanding features of my stay
at Redding. I had fun playing the games, I enjoyed the society of Frances and the dolls; and I relished the hours in the
sunshiny loggia hearing Mr. Clemens read aloud, as well as
romping with Tammany and the new kittens she had just presented to the household. But most of all I loved the walks
with Mr. Clemens, when the Authors' League flourished in
the abstract, even though not a single line was written.

I had ten days with Mark Twain at Redding—ten beautiful
days, replete with so many good things that the remembrance
of them crowded each other out. Then the time came when
I had to say good-by.

Mother and I were to visit friends in New Hampshire, and the time planned for our visit had come so we had to leave "Innocence at Home." I didn't want to go and Mr. Clemens was urging us to stay, but we had promised to go to New Hampshire and were expected. So there was nothing to do but pack our bags.

But, as usual, I had the prospect of coming back to Redding. Mr. Clemens insisted that I must visit him before my school started again, which, of course, was a joy to anticipate. Mr. Clemens said he wanted to have a couple of his angelfishes under his roof all the time, and I must come back as often as I could, and we definitely planned for at least a week's visit later on.

So I drove away waving my hand to Mr. Clemens, who was standing between the arches of the loggia waving to us. He had a smile on his lips, and was calling out gay messages. The last I heard was "Come again, you little rat," and then we were beyond the sound of his low voice; but for a long way down the winding road I could see his white-clad figure, staunch and upright, with the sunlight throwing golden glints on his shock of white hair and the arm that was still waving to me.

This was a sight that I have never forgotten, for it etched itself upon my memory. For some reason I cherished that glimpse of him close to my heart, even though I had no idea that many, many months were to pass before I would see him again and that when I did he would be quite different from the gay and happy person I had left in the loggia of his new home that August day.

Mother and I went straight to Epping, New Hampshire, when we left Redding, and I, of course, wrote Mr. Clemens at once and told him what a wonderful time I had had visiting him. Later I had a letter from him.

INNOCENCE AT HOME
REDDING, CONNECTICUT
Aug. 12/08

Dorothy dear,

I wrote you a number of days ago, and mailed it to Epping, but I don't think you'll get it, because I couldn't make sure of the address you gave me. If it is Dow, you should write it like this: DOW—not like this dow (which is the way you wrote it). Don't ever again write a proper name in any but CAPITALS—do you hear?

But you'll never get this, so why should I go on writing?

With lots of love,
SLC

I had received the letter he mentioned, on the outside of the envelope of which he had written, "You careless little rascal, why don't you write addresses plainer? SLC." This had greatly intrigued the tiny Epping post office employees. They had, of course, known whom it was from, for there was a printed "S. L. Clemens, Redding, Connecticut" in the corner.

His letters were full of the things he was doing, so that I never for one moment felt out of touch with the big house on the hill. SLC always kept me fully informed about what was going on, and I read his letter proudly to the house party; after a while the assembled guests watched the mails for them as eagerly as I did.

I didn't get back to Redding before school opened. The New Hampshire air seemed to agree with me so well that Mother kept me there until just before time for school; even Mr. Clemens agreed that it was obviously the thing to do as I hadn't had a single attack of bronchitis.

We did plan to stop off at Redding for a few days on our way down, but just then Mr. Clemens was called away on business so the visit had to be postponed until the holidays. Just as SLC had foreseen, I couldn't go to "Innocence at Home" as I had gone to No. 21 Fifth Avenue. The trip was much too long from Plainfield to Redding, and now my studies were more advanced. I couldn't miss Monday morning at the seminary. I had to keep my nose buried in my books; but I did send my little stories back and forth and was always very happy when SLC said my style was improving.

In October the new house was broken into by burglars. I read long accounts of it in the paper but almost immediately received a letter from Mr. Clemens in which he treated the episode very lightly. "Burglars broke in after midnight this morning," he said, "but they were caught afterwards and are on their way to jail this afternoon."

Mr. Clemens was very bold and brave about the matter, but the rest of the household apparently were affected a little differently, for a few days later he wrote again:

INNOCENCE AT HOME
REDDING, CONNECTICUT
October 7/08

How are you getting along, dear heart? The Women Folks in this house are not getting along well at all. Their sleep is broken and is pestered with dreadful dreams every night. I mean about burglars. Catherine says she has the same dream every night, in which a swarm of masked burglars are riddling her with bullets. It fetches her out of her slumbers with a shriek.

We've built a garage. It was necessary, for the Sunday morning train was taken off. Actors cannot come to us now save by motor car. They can fetch it by train to S. Norwalk and motor the rest of the way in less than an hour.

We are putting glass in the arches of the loggia and turning it into a Winter parlor so that we can sit there with our knitting and watch the snowstorms. We have plenty of cats and kittens now—all descendants of the incomparable Tammany.

SLC

I was sure from that letter that there had been no repercussions from the excitement for him anyway. It must have been a very "nervous business," as SLC himself would have put it, for the two burglars were discovered making off with the family silver. Claude, the butler, shot his revolver to thoroughly frighten them off. It is just as well that he did so, for he not only saved the silver but probably serious consequences, for they were pretty desperate men and later when they were captured shot one of the officers.

I didn't know that at the time of the event Mr. Clemens, who had been asleep and was awakened by the shots, thought some champagne was being opened and promptly sank back into his slumbers. And though the rest of the household were considerably wrought up, he apparently was not disturbed even after he knew what had been going on.

In fact, he tacked a notice on the front door for the next robbers that might appear, cautioning them not to make a noise as it disturbed the family, and telling them where the plated ware they now used could be found. He wound up by asking them to please close the door when they left.

At first Mr. Clemens had thought he might return to No. 21 Fifth Avenue for part of the winter; then as he spent more time at Redding, he liked it better and better and decided not to come back to town any more. He said that he loved the free, open life of the country and that he was just going to enjoy himself doing the things he liked from now on—and being in the country was one of them.

One day when I was in town riding up Fifth Avenue, I saw signs of occupancy at No. 21. At first my heart almost stopped with joy, for my initial thought was that SLC had come back. But when I considered it I knew this couldn't be, for Mother reminded me that only a day or so before I had had a letter from Mr. Clemens expressing his complete satisfaction with Redding as a residence. So I came down to earth and realized the house must be rented.

Since I owed Mr. Clemens a letter, I wrote and told him of the incident and asked if I were right. At the same time I said that I had just read in the paper that there had been another robbery at his house and that a great many of his own books had been stolen. I chided him for not having told me of this second attempt.

A few days later came his answer to both questions.

REDDING, CONNECTICUT
Nov. 5/08

Dear heart,

I said last night, "I'll write a letter in the morning and give a certain Dorothy a scolding and inquire what has become of her." So you have spoken up just in time to save yourself.

Yes, No. 21 is rented and occupied. We shan't leave Redding any more, Winter or Summer. We like it here better and better all the time.

Dear, I haven't heard of the second robbery. If it was only books of mine that were stolen and not Bibles, I am glad, for the robbers will read those books and become good citizens and valuable men —but they wouldn't read Bibles.

It is a pity you lost the cat, but I can sympathize with you for we have ourselves suffered a heavy loss in that line. Tammany is dead; killed by a dog, we think, when she was out hunting. She was the finest cat and the handsomest in America. Moreover, she was an officer of the Aquarium. I appointed her myself. She was the Aquarium's mascAT and brought it good luck as long as she lived. We buried her with the honors due her rank.

In token of respect for her memory and regret for her loss, it is requested that each M. A. shall wear black head ribbons during one hour of the 30th of this month, Tammany's birthday. See that you obey.

SLC

My own regret over my little cat that had strayed away was quite swallowed in grief for Tammany, for whom I had had a real affection. The cat whose leaving I had reported to Mr. Clemens I had not had long enough to grow very attached to, but Tammany, whom I had played with and loved, who had been so much a part of those happy times at No. 21, was a real loss. I wore the black hair ribbon as SLC had said, and at the same time truly mourned that my furry friend was no longer curled up on the hearth of "Innocence at Home."

29

Home Becomes "Stormfield,"
and SLC Is Ill

I WORKED VERY HARD at school so that when I went to Redding during the Christmas holidays I would have a good report to make to SLC. I found that it is easy to do good work when you are striving to please someone.

When the vacation came I had a good report—yes, even for arithmetic—but I also had the bronchitis, which was definitely not good for me or my prospects for a visit. I spent the holidays in bed, and sent my Christmas present to Mr. Clemens instead of taking it myself as I had planned.

He sent me another angelfish pin, a much larger one than the badge of the Aquarium. I was very happy over it, but lovely as it was it didn't make up for my disappointment in not seeing my friend.

For a Happy New Year's greeting he sent me a colored post card of the house, which he had renamed "Stormfield." Why the change of name had been made, I didn't know, for he had been very pleased with "Innocence at Home." He had declared it to be the right name for the house, and while it bore that name, it was a happy, carefree house, the house of gaiety and joy. Later, when the name was altered, it became a house of storm and stress, tragedy and tears. There is a psychology and a power in names. The old Egyptians knew it. Mr. Clemens, himself, had told me of their words of magic that they hardly dared to speak and if they did, used only the lowest whisper. Mr. Clemens knew, too.

In his very first talk with me he had said, "Words are very important things," and he reiterated the fact over and over in "Adam's Diary." Still he altered the name of the house to "Stormfield," and it proved an unfortunate change. I always meant to ask him why but never did. At the time I supposed it was because the house, set on a high knoll, was in the midst of a field and because Redding produced the most terrific thunderstorms. It was what the Zulus would have called a "place-of-the-thunders-meeting." Mr. Clemens often wrote describing the storms he was watching from the loggia. It wasn't until years after when I was reading Mr. Paine's wonderful biography that I learned the reason for the change. Mr. Paine said that Mr. Clemens had for some time been considering a new name, although he always meant to retain "Innocence at Home" for the Angel Fishes. For a while he thought of "Stormfield," for part of the house had been built with the money *Captain Stormfield's Visit to Heaven* had brought him, but it wasn't until one day when he had watched a storm sweeping down over the hills and fields that he gave it the new appellation, "Stormfield."

So now his paper had "STORMFIELD, REDDING, CONNECTICUT," and it was in black print, not the gay red I had so much admired.

Later that winter Mr. Clemens, who had been struggling

with bronchitis, as well as I, was ordered to Bermuda, and wrote asking me to come, repeating, "In Bermuda you won't need any medicines." He wrote Mother too, urging her to bring me, but this was out of the question for I was in bed practically all the time he was away. When I finally did get better, the family decided to take me to Europe the minute school was over, since the long sea voyage did me a great deal of good and I was rarely ill in Europe. So I wrote Mr. Clemens that I was going and wouldn't be back until late fall, and he replied:

Stormfield

March 3/09
Well, dear, so you're going abroad in June. The very best month for it. If I were sixty years younger, I would pack my grip and go along with you. Louise Paine, M. A., went abroad a fortnight ago—her first trip—and she was wild with delight. She went with her father who is my biographer, and they will go over the ground I travelled in the *Innocents Abroad* forty-two years ago, and make notes.

Dorothy Bates, M. A. is coming abroad (to visit me, she is a Londoner) next August. Francesca, M. A. is going abroad in June. Helen Marlin, M. A. will go abroad in May. Dorothy Harvey, M. A., has already gone abroad. It's a frisk-about lot, my angel fishes. I can't keep enough of them in the tank to make a show.

Then he went on to tell me of his visitors and what good times they had been having, until I was filled with a nostalgic longing to be one of them and to see my friend again. It seemed almost as though fate had been placing obstacles in the path of our being together, but no separation could alter the love I had for him. There is nothing so deep and sincere as the affection of a child. Children's likes and dislikes are very real personal things, and all the more intense because they are completely natural. Children either like you or they do not. When they do, it is a compliment, for you, yourself, have won them. I adored SLC, and whether I saw him or not, there was nothing that could disturb my feeling for him.

During the time I was in Europe, there wasn't anything that gave me so much joy as the letters that came from Mark Twain. They were always full of news of his activities and his visitors.

"We sat in the loggia reading and talking and enjoying the wonderful day with someone at the orchestrelle much of the time."

His words would set me on a magic carpet of thoughts that flew back over the ocean to Redding, until I felt as though I were actually there, I could see the picture so clearly.

A quite usual ending to his letters would be, "Hearts will begin in ten minutes from now, so I will go downstairs and be ready." He would even tell me the score of the last game, and I noticed that he was still winning! And even in the midst of the fascinating things I was doing, the age-old wonders I was seeing, I would feel a pang of homesickness for the long, low house and its gentle owner, and wish I were beside him.

But, since that could not be, I wrote long accounts of my own adventures, which he greatly enjoyed and kept urging me to write even more fully, "Because it is such good practice for you."

Then there came quite a gap in his letters. I didn't hear from him for a long time, which seemed even longer because I was so far away. At last arrived a post card of Stormfield. He had written on its back and enclosed it in an envelope. It was the first news I had had of his illness.

Dorothy dear,

I've been intending to write you this good while but I am on the sick list and can't very well do things. I went to Baltimore June 8 and the journey and the weather together broke me down. I haven't had a well day since. Lately I keep to my room almost all the time and I don't like the confinement much. A journey to New York last August gave me my first setback, but I soon got over that one. I shall get over this one by and by, but not right away. The old saw says, 'Go it while you're young,' and that is what I advise you to do, dear.

SLC

I felt badly to think that SLC had been ill, but I wasn't particularly alarmed. In the course of my various attacks of bronchitis, being confined to my room was an everyday affair. So it didn't strike me as seriously as it should have done. I remembered the attack he spoke of "last August." He had gone down to New York from Redding on business and had written me that the heat and the stifling city air in contrast to the cool, life-giving atmosphere of the country had brought on a bilious attack, and he would never, never go to New York in the summer again. I recalled that perfectly and that he had gotten over it without a great deal of discomfort, and I thought this attack would be the same.

Even though I received more messages on post cards than I did letters, I still wasn't alarmed. But when, just before we sailed for home, I had another card with a more serious message upon it, I was frightened.

Sept. 10/09

Dear Dorothy,

I am glad to hear you are enjoying yourself. I am still a prisoner in the house these past three months with no prospect of getting out for a long, long time to come. But I guess it's all right. Infirmities and disabilities are quite proper to old age. Have a good time while you're young, dear.

With lots of love,

SLC

It was the beginning of Stormfield's casting its shadow—if such things can be.

Child though I was, I could read through the lines. His other cards and letters had been deceivingly gay, because he didn't want me to worry, I am sure; but in this last message his wistfulness crept through, along with the truth about himself. He had been indoors for three months. That, to me, meant more than bronchitis, even though I was too young to realize the real seriousness of the implication. I never thought of him as old. To me he was ever youthful, despite his good-natured chaffing over being elderly. But I was miserable at the idea of SLC's being inactive. He was always so vibrantly alert, so full of the keenest enjoyment of even the simplest pleasures, that it just didn't seem right that he should be deprived of them for even a short time, let alone three weary months.

I concentrated all my wishes into one, that he would soon be well, and daily prayed for the same thing. And it seemed as though my efforts were rewarded, for toward the end of November, Mark Twain was much better and wrote that he was looking forward to a wonderful Christmas with his daughter Jean, at home to share it with him and to rejoice in his good health.

30

"No Matter What Happens,
You Must Write"

THE FIRST PART OF DECEMBER, when he was feeling better, the old dry humor which had been lacking while he was ill returned to his letters. I had written him about the death of my bird "Happy," whom he had heard so much about that he felt he knew her—just as I had felt thoroughly acquainted with the last lot of Tammany's kittens, even though I had never been introduced to them except by mail. So when I reported Happy's sad demise from old age, and the fact that I had been given a new canary as an advance Christmas gift, he wrote:

STORMFIELD

December 10/09

I am sorry, Dorothy dear, that your old bird died and glad you've got a fresh one. I know it is a pretty one for by your description of it I recognize it as a bird I am very well acquainted with. It is a chicken hawk and is one of the finest of the feathered singers. I used to have one and when it was not catching chickens and cats, it would sit around and sing by the hour. It was a delight to everyone on the place. I hope you will get the other one all in good time.

Irene's bird is dead. It was a beautiful creature. She got it in Bermuda when we were there a year ago. That is one of the main troubles about pets—one gets very fond of them, then they die and break your heart.

I'm not going to Bermuda this season. I have now spent six Summer months here and shall stay right here along until Winter comes. That will be about next July, I reckon, the way things look.

Life is very strange. When he wrote consoling me about my pet he had no idea that fifteen days later his heart would be broken by the tragic death of his daughter Jean, on Christmas Eve—all the more heart-rending because she had been making such high plans for a Merry Christmas for him, and trimming the large tree was the last thing she had done. She had also arranged for the village children to come in on Christmas Day and sing carols to the orchestrelle's accompaniment, and had gone up to her room in the best of spirits.

The shock of her sudden passing was a terrific one for Mr. Clemens in his frail state of health. He had been so happy to have Jean home again and well after all the years she had suffered ill health, that it was all the harder, especially since Clara was abroad on her honeymoon. The marriage of Clara Clemens and Ossip Gabrilówitsch had taken place at Redding that fall and had greatly pleased Mr. Clemens.

When Jean was taken away from him, he bore the blow magnificently, but it took away all the progress he had made.

I wrote him the minute I heard the sad news, but I had no reply. I used often to look at the post card he had sent me two days before Christmas, "Love and Merry Christmas to

Dorothy, SLC," for it was the last line I had had from him. I was unhappy for him and could hardly do my lessons wondering how he was.

Mr. Paine wrote a very kind letter saying that Mr. Clemens wanted to thank me for my sympathy which meant so much to him, and that he was going to Bermuda and hoped I would come to visit him when he returned. Then there was a silence during which SLC struggled with sorrow and illness. But in Bermuda he rallied and wrote and urged me to come down. He had followed his own prescription and wanted to share it with his friend.

I had been ill myself, my old enemy bronchitis having played games with me all winter, so the doctors said I would have to give up school for the time being and get back my strength. Bermuda seemed an ideal spot for that and I wanted to see Mr. Clemens again more than anything in the world, so this time his urging was not in vain.

The first part of March found me on my way to the lovely islands. I had wired Mr. Clemens I was coming, and just after I arrived at the Hamilton Hotel, I saw his white-clad figure striding through the lobby. He went toward the desk, but before he had time to inquire for us, I ran to meet him and for a few minutes the joy of our reunion swept all thoughts of sorrow away.

It didn't seem possible that almost a year and a half had gone by since I had seen him. The intervening months seemed to have slipped away, and Mark Twain and I met on the same plane of companionship that we had always shared.

That is one of the greatest tests of friendship; a true one remains unaltered through the application of any test, even the acid one of time. Ours had come through unchanged. It was as though we had parted yesterday.

But he was a changed Mr. Clemens in other ways. He looked his age for the first time. In fact, he seemed suddenly to have grown years older and very worn. The once erect figure was a little stooped. He no longer threw back his chest, but the old flame was in his eyes when they met mine.

I had changed, too. I had always been tall for my age, but in the last year I had shot up several inches. My head was much over his shoulder now.

Hand in hand, we went over to where Mother was waiting; then we found seats in a quiet corner and sat there for a long time. He continued to hold my hand close while he told me how happy he was that we were in Bermuda together at last, for now we would be able to do all the things he had spoken of so often and have lots of good times together.

He even said, "We must start the Authors' League again. Now that I am feeling better, I must look into what progress you've made."

I had to confess that without his guiding hand I hadn't been inspired to make any literary efforts.

He shook his head sadly and wisely. "No matter what happens, Dorothy dear, you must write: cataclysms, sorrow, pain, nothing must interfere with the expression of a talent that should have its outlet. A trade that is once taken up must be followed to the bitter end. It's your job in life and you must see that it is well done."

His eyes were half-closed as he spoke, and it seemed as though he were talking more to himself than to me. Nevertheless, I promised I would start work again, though he said I didn't need to promise, for he would see I kept at it.

The hours went so quickly that it was almost time for dinner before we realized it. When Mr. Clemens finally noticed that it was getting late, he announced regretfully that he would have to go as he was staying with some friends. He said his hostess, a Mrs. Allen, would call Mrs. Quick very soon as they wanted her and Dorothy to come to tea the following Sunday.

Finally he left. I walked to the door with him and saw him drive off in one of the open victorias for which Bermuda was noted. As he waved good-by, I wanted to rush out and go with him, for it didn't seem natural that we should not be together.

However, it wasn't a long separation, for that evening he returned with Helen, the daughter of his hostess. I was happily surprised, for he had explained that he wasn't going out at nights at all. But he must have had the same feeling I had had when I wanted to rush out to the carriage and take my usual place at his side, for he said, "Knowing you were so near, I just felt I had to see you. We've been separated so long that now I've actually got you in Bermuda, I don't want to lose a second of your companionship."

Nothing could have made me happier. We had some chairs placed where we could watch the dancing and had a very pleasant evening. When Mr. Clemens introduced me to Woodrow Wilson, who happened to pass by, I felt that the old times were getting off to a good start. Wasn't I already meeting celebrities? Mr. Wilson was president of Princeton at the time and was in Bermuda for a short holiday with his wife.

SLC's comments on the dancers made me feel even more that the clock had been turned back.

"See that man?" he pointed. "He dances more like a jumping jack, loose and wobbly but with an incessant motion."

One had only to see the dancer to fully appreciate the humor of the remark.

As it grew late, Mark Twain said, "Dorothy, you've grown so much I almost forgot you have an early bedtime."

214

I quickly told him my hour of retiring was very unimportant compared to being with him, and my wise and understanding Mother did not contradict me. But Mr. Clemens shook his head. There was a wistfulness in his voice as he replied, and a little sadness. "Well, I'm not as young as you, dear, and I have to keep my hours. But I'll see you tomorrow and I will bring Mrs. Allen who personally wants to invite my little friend and her Mother to tea." It seemed to me as he spoke that his drawl was slower and more exaggerated than ever.

He came back the next afternoon as he had promised, and while Mrs. Allen, a very charming woman, talked to Mother, SLC and I had a grand time reviving all the good times we had had in the past until he appeared as animated and gay as the Mark Twain of No. 21 Fifth Avenue had been. Finally he rose to go and with his arm around my shoulder said, "I will see you tomorrow, dear heart, and we will have such good times together."

"We will have good times," I repeated, as I kissed him good-by, little dreaming that this was the last time I was to see his kindly, gentle face with the drooping moustache and the blue eyes framed by his soft, white hair.

The next day was rainy and Mr. Clemens sent a note to the hotel by Claude, whom he had brought to Bermuda with him as a valet. In it he explained that since he had a slight cold he had to keep to his room and couldn't come to see me, nor would he risk my catching it by letting me come to him. But he said he would get well and surely see me Sunday, if not before, and we would have plenty of opportunity for our good times as we were both staying on for several weeks.

But the good times were not to be. On Saturday morning Mother received a cable that her brother had died very suddenly, and she and I had to return at once.

The boat we had come down on was out in the harbor just ready to sail, but the hotel manager had it held for us and we were taken out to it in a launch; the tender had already left.

In the excitement of getting off, I scribbled a note to SLC while Mother was packing, but through some carelessness on the part of the hotel, it never got to him, so that quite a while after I had reached home I heard from him:

> BAY HOUSE, HAMILTON
> March 10/1910
> Sunday

Dorothy Dear,

I am so sorry to hear the sad news that hurries you and your Mother home. Yesterday you did not come to us, and we wondered if something was wrong. I could not go out at night yet, and had been shut up with my cough since Wednesday morning—a fresh accession to it—so I sent my man servant to inquire, and he brought word from the hotel that you had received a cable that your uncle was very ill and you had taken ship at once. The world seems full of trouble for us all.

The young people came yesterday afternoon, after the rain, and played tennis, but I did not go outdoors; I was out Thursday afternoon and played a game, but had a hard night to pay for it. This is now the fourth day that Helen has been in bed, and I think her Mother *ought* to have been in bed yesterday, but she stayed up to take care of the company. All this illness comes of my catching a cold in the head three weeks ago from a visitor who brought it from America. The household caught it from me. Mine ran into bronchitis.

The Colliers arrived last Friday, but I only learned it this evening, for they sent me no word and will have to be scolded. Mr. Collier is ailing—the New York Winter has been too much for him.

I am so sorry you had to go away, for I think a few weeks' rest in this climate would be good for you, Dear.

216

Please give your mother my kindest regards. With lots of love,

SLC

Apparently they had kept the extent of the bad news we had received from Mr. Clemens, fearing it might depress him. SLC was right when he said, "The world seems full of trouble for us all." When his letter reached me I was indeed full of trouble, for not only had I lost my uncle, but Mother was very ill from the shock of his sudden passing.

As soon as Mother recovered my grandparents took us to Europe, and it was while we were in London that the papers blazed forth the news that Mark Twain was dead. He had battled with sickness until he could fight no more.

While the whole world mourned his passing, a little girl shed bitter tears, bitter tears for the SLC she had loved with all her heart. Even though I read the long accounts of his passing and his funeral, it just didn't seem possible that that bright, shining star had set.

I know better now. I know that it can never set, that although we can no longer see it in the heavens, the light from its radiance still permeates the world in the tangible evidences of himself that he left behind him—for the spirit of Mark Twain is eternal.

When I read that he "went peacefully to sleep on a bright, sunshiny Spring day," I remembered how much he and the sunshine had been a part of my life, and I was inconsolable.

There is no grief so deep that time does not lessen it. No passage of days can ever erase love, but it can and mercifully does numb the sense of loss. It did so for me, but I couldn't write any more. The Authors' League had ceased to be; my inspiration was gone. So I put away my notebooks and tried to forget.

For many years I refused to let the idea of writing come back into my thoughts. I studied singing after I graduated from school with the idea of an operatic career, for there was an urge in me that demanded some medium of expression. But all the time there was a murmur in the back of my mind, a whispering that would not be silent, for the memory of what Mark Twain had said kept drawing me back to the thing he had wanted me to do. Like the recurrent pull of the undertow, it was ever present in the depths of my being, and I could not shut it away.

So at last I got out the old notebooks and Mark Twain's letters that had been packed away so long, and as I reread them they opened my mind to the urge and made me realize that to ease my own sorrow I had selfishly betrayed the faith SLC had had in me. I remembered he had said, "No matter what happens, you must write," and I made up my mind that I would justify this faith to the best of my ability, and although I might never realize it, I would at least have followed the path he had chosen for me.

So I began to write again—slowly, stumblingly, without a guide, but with rich memories of Mark Twain's friendship and his interest in me to spur me on.

31

Epilogue

WRITING THIS BOOK, I have often felt like Alice In Wonderland, especially at that moment when, after she drank the bottle in the rabbit's house, she had suddenly grown very big and looked at her feet a long, long way off, and wondered if they were really hers. I, too, have looked a long way off, toward the little girl who was, and in some strange incomprehensible way, still is, me.

I have tried to write this book through the little girl's eyes, not through my own grown-up ones, because I felt that only that way could I give the right picture of the Mark Twain I knew and loved—the portrait that I am sure is what he would want. "Show me as I was, Dorothy, the real me," I can almost hear his slow, drawly voice saying. So I have written the story of his friendship for me, and in reliving those happy days I have had so much pleasure myself that I hope a little of it creeps through the printed pages to whoever may read them.

I only wish I could have produced a book that Mr. Clemens would have been able to say "well done" about, even though in the next breath he told me to rewrite it—for practice!

I *have* rewritten many parts, and even now I do not feel I have said quite all I wanted to say, nor that I have been able to pay him quite the tribute that I wanted to, because words are difficult things to manage when it comes to expressing one's innermost feelings, and even the best of them are inadequate at revealing deep and sincere emotions.

Writing this, I have stepped back of the mirror of the present into the past and relived days that were full of joy and color. I have brought back happenings of long ago that have been resting undisturbed in some locked cupboard of my mind until it seems as though it were only yesterday when a little girl sat at the feet of a great man and learned—many things.

The whole world of letters has cause to be grateful to Mark Twain. He was the one writer who brought humor—the real, vibrant "joy of living" mirth—to its height in literature. He blazed the pathway in which so many others have followed. He gave a great store of books to America; his has been a great name to look up to and be proud of and to pattern after, although no one can ever quite reach the peaks he touched.

To have known him as I did was a rare gift which, as the years go by, I appreciate more and more fully. Just to have revolved in his radius for a few brief years was an unforgettable privilege. To have had his love and his interest, his faith that I would accomplish something, was even greater, and the desire to fulfill his hopes for me will always remain an integral part of my being—a goal I will strive constantly to achieve.

But one thing is certain, whether I make a success of writing or not; Mark Twain brought more into the life of this little girl than anyone could guess. Entirely apart from the literary angle, the influence of a man like Mark Twain in a child's life is incalculable. I don't know how the other Angel Fish feel, but I am sure it must be the same with them as it is with me. For the time we knew him we lived in a rarefied atmosphere in which all things of life seemed to assume their true and proper proportions. We learned the simplicity of the great and the unassumption of the rich and true heart that held honor before everything and exalted right thinking and living to its highest degree.

The very fact of having been in such an atmosphere cannot help but clear the lungs of the murky dust of everyday life; it cannot help but give an incentive to carry on—to try to be as noble and as fine as he was in every way.

And that is a heritage that Mark Twain has not only given to me, who loved him, but to the whole world.